From Birdbrained to Brilliant

Training the Sporting Dog to be a Great Companion

Dawn Antoniak-Mitchell, CPDT-KSA, CBCC-KA

Wenatchee, Washington U.S.A.

From Birdbrained to Brilliant
Training the Sporting Dog to be a Great Companion
Dawn Antoniak-Mitchell, CPDT-KSA, CBCC-KA

Dogwise Publishing
A Division of Direct Book Service, Inc.
403 South Mission Street, Wenatchee, Washington 98801
1-509-663-9115, 1-800-776-2665
www.dogwisepublishing.com / info@dogwisepublishing.com

Graphic design: Lindsay Peternell
Cover design: Lindsay Peternell
Cover photo: Jayme Nelson
On the cover: Carla Slabaugh and her Vizsla called Brock whose fully titled name is:
GCH Am/Int'l CH Sokoldalu-N-Tierah's Total Power Package BN RN JH OAJ NA
(www.SokoldaluVizslas.com)

Library of Congress Cataloging-in-Publication Data
Antoniak-Mitchell, Dawn, 1966-
  From birdbrained to brilliant : training the sporting dog to be a great companion / Dawn Antoniak-Mitchell, CPDT-KSA, CBCC-KA.
    pages cm
  Includes index.
  ISBN 978-1-61781-137-1
  1. Hunting dogs--Training. I. Title.
  SF428.5.A58 2014
  636.75--dc23
                                              2013045266

ISBN: 978-1-61781-137-1

Printed in the U.S.A.

To my Curly-Coated Retriever muses,
Shocker and Barnum.

You taught me well the joy
inherent in every stick.

Table of Contents

Acknowledgments

Thank you once again to everyone at Dogwise for their help and encouragement with this book. My learning curve was not as steep this time in large part because of all the help you gave me on my last project.

Thank you to my parents and grandparents for instilling in me a respect for all living things, a desire to pursue excellence, and a passion for learning. Without these traits, I would not have walked down the life path I have enjoyed so much. And to Jeff, for walking the majority of that path hand-in-hand with me.

Thank you to all the BonaFide Dog Academy students and their dogs and my fellow dog trainers the world over who graciously helped me create many of the photographs for this book. And a big thank you to Doris Hodges and Kaija Braid for helping me make connections I could not have possibly made on my own. I am honored to know all of you and your awesome sporting dogs!

This book, like the previous one, builds on the works of many respected scientists, trainers, animal behaviorists, and dog breeders. Many of the exercises and games in this book are adaptations of ideas from well-known trainers such as Karen Pryor, Patricia McConnell, Brenda Aloff, Leslie McDevitt, Turid Rugaas, and Sylvia Bishop, as well as lesser-known, but equally talented, trainers and sporting dog fanciers of the past and present, such as Jim Barry, S. T. Hammond, and many others. Thank you to all who have taken the time over the years to share their knowledge and expertise with others for the benefit of our dogs.

And, as always, the biggest debt of gratitude I owe is to the generations of sporting dog owners the world over who created, adapted, protected, and passed down these wonderful dog breeds to us. The continued popularity of these dogs as both workers and companions is a testament to the success of their efforts.

Introduction

You can know the name of a bird in all the languages of the world, but when you're finished, you'll know absolutely nothing whatever about the bird... So let's look at the bird and see what it's doing—that's what counts. I learned very early the difference between knowing the name of something and knowing something.

~ Richard Feynman
American physicist

There are many excellent books and training classes out there that cover the mechanics of teaching any breed of dog basic obedience skills, such as how to sit, lie down, or walk politely on a leash. The purpose of this book is to give you training exercises, management techniques, and games that are specifically designed to help you, as a sporting dog owner (or prospective owner), address the unique training challenges that often come with opening your heart and home to a sporting dog. Too often, owners get frustrated with normal sporting dog behavior and resort to either heavy-handed, ineffective training tactics, or simply give up and accept inappropriate behaviors as a necessary part of life with their dogs. This book will show you how to develop a loving, positive, working relationship with your canine companion by working *with* your sporting dog's instincts, rather than *against* them, to teach him how to behave appropriately in your home.

Although you can certainly skip the history and learning theory chapters and jump right into the training exercises, you will be doing yourself and your dog a disservice if you do. Even though most of us consider our dogs to be members of our families, we need to remember no matter how much we love them, they are still dogs, not furry little humans. They are beautiful, fascinating, intelligent, funny, irritating, independent, loyal, loving, entertaining, unique beings, but they are definitely *not* human. They are dogs. And they aren't just any type of dog either; they are *sporting dogs*. We need to understand and appreciate the similarities and differences between humans and dogs to have a positive relationship with them. And we need to understand and appreciate the similarities and differences between sporting dogs and other breeds of dogs so we can effectively teach them how we expect them to behave in our modern world.

In this book, we will explore how modern sporting dog breeds came into being and how the sporting dog's ancestral work still affects sporting dog behavior today. We will then look at learning theory and the proper use of reinforcement to learn how to most effectively train our dogs. Finally, we will consider what we really should be teaching our sporting dogs so that they can enjoy fulfilling lives in our modern human society. By developing a sporting dog-centric view of the world, we can better help our sporting dogs reach their full potential as the wonderful companions they can be.

For those who have read *Terrier-Centric Dog Training: From Tenacious to Tremendous*, you may notice there are several similar exercises found in both books. While some of the exercises themselves may be the same, the purpose behind teaching them to both working terriers and sporting dogs is not. For example, The Eyes Have It teaches a dog to give eye contact on cue and is an important exercise to teach sporting dogs, as well as working terriers, but for very different reasons. Both types of dogs, as part of their historical work, were developed to be alert to the movement of animals. A working terrier and a sporting dog are naturally apt to notice and pay attention to animals moving in their environs, including an approaching dog and person. However, because these breeds were developed for two radically different types of work, the typical consequences of allowing a working terrier to stare at an approaching dog, as compared to allowing a sporting dog to stare, are rarely the same. Working terriers were bred to harass and kill vermin, usually with little or no help from their handlers or other dogs, while sporting dogs were bred to work under close control of hunters and sometimes with other dogs to locate quarry and recover dead or injured game animals. As a result of these historical breed differences, a working terrier that is allowed to stare at another dog may instinctively get mentally and physically prepared to fight, simply because he is hard-wired to react decisively to the slightest perceived threat from any other animal, while the sporting dog may get excited and uncontrollable because of his social instincts to work with other dogs and people. Both responses are equally inappropriate and can trigger a potentially dangerous response from the approaching dog if the situation isn't defused quickly and calmly. One way to handle the situation is to ask your dog to look at you, instead of the approaching dog and person, to help your dog maintain self-control. Teaching eye contact on cue may very well be the training that keeps a working terrier from becoming so aroused he tries to fight with another dog and keeps a sporting dog from becoming so goofy happy he tries to kill another dog with kindness. From a behavioral viewpoint, these are two very different reactions that are being prevented simply by redirecting what the dogs are allowed to look at. But from a training standpoint, both types of dogs can be taught the same basic behavior to accomplish the goal of redirecting their attention. Chapter 2 will examine in greater detail the similarities and differences in behavior between sporting dogs and other types of dogs. Chapters 4 and 10 will further explain why being overly-friendly is just as unacceptable as being overly-grumpy when it comes to canine interactions. So while there is definitely some overlap in training exercises between the two books, the instinct-based reasons behind teaching different types of dogs the same or similar exercises are quite different. And it is understanding these instinctual differences between sporting dogs and other types of dogs, and how to work with those instincts to help our sporting dogs become the best companions they can be, that the rest of this book is devoted.

Chapter 1

What Exactly is a Sporting Dog?

The dog is the only animal that is capable of disinterested affection. He is the only one that regards the human being as his companion, and follows him as his friend; the only one that seems to possess a natural desire to be useful to him, from a spontaneous impulse attached himself to man. We take the bridle from the mouth of the horse, and turn him free into the pasture, and he testifies his joy in his partially recovered liberty. We exact from the dog the service that is required of him, and he still follows us. He solicits to be continued as our companion and our friend.

~ William Youatt
The Dog

Dogs and humans have lived together for thousands of years. Although scientists continue to argue over exactly how and why domestic dogs first came into existence, they all agree that soon after dogs were domesticated, humans began to develop different types of dogs to hunt, guard, herd, draft, and perform other specialized tasks to help man survive and thrive throughout the world. The dogs we own today still possess most of the carefully selected physical traits and instincts of their ancestors. These traits and instincts impact their behavior, whether or not our dogs actually still perform their ancestral breed jobs. Understanding the traits and instincts that are likely to appear in our sporting dogs is the first step toward developing a sporting dog-centric training program that will help us train our dogs in a positive, effective, fun way for us and our dogs.

Sporting dog history in a nutshell

As humans began relying on dogs to help find and capture game, they also began refining breeds to address the local needs of hunters. Different types of game and different types of terrain demanded different types of hunting dogs. Technology also greatly influenced the development of the modern gun dog breeds. In ancient times, hunting dogs primarily caught and killed game on their own. Breeds were later developed to be used together with nets, snares, and falcons to aid the hunter. But most of the modern sporting dog breeds we are familiar with didn't fully develop until after the modern hunting gun that could be operated by a single hunter was invented. According to William Arkwright in his book *The Pointer and His Predecessors*, the ancestry of the modern hunting gun dates back to the *harquebus*, an obsolete 16th century firearm which could be shot from a stationary position, and later, the German *platine á rouet* (the flint lock gun), which allowed mobile shooting (bibliographic information on cited works in the body of the text may be found in the Resources section at the back of the book). By 1620, firearms had sufficiently developed to allow for relatively easy handling and by 1750, double-barrel guns became available for hunters to use. With the invention of this gun, the era of the modern gun dog breeds began.

British breed historian Hugh Dalziel divided sporting dogs into four broad groups in his influential 19th-century book *British Dogs—Their Varieties, History, Characteristics, Breeding, Management and Exhibition:* "Division I—Dogs used in field sports. Group I—Those that pursue and kill their game, depending entirely or mainly on sight and speed... Group II—Those hunting their game by scent and killing it... Group III—Those that find the game by scent, but trained to forego their natural instinct to pursue, and to stand and index the game for the advantage of the gun... Group IV—Other varieties used with the gun in questing and retrieving...." These groups were based on the work the dogs performed, rather than artificial divisions arising from physical appearance. Although Dalziel wrote about breeds known at the time in the British Isles, these groups apply to sporting dogs used world-wide and provide a useful framework for considering the similarities and differences between different types of sporting dogs. Each group has a unique hunting style, and within each group, individual breeds were refined to meet specific local hunting needs.

Groups I and II consist of sporting breeds which historically did not work closely with humans in the pursuit of prey and usually killed the prey once it was overtaken, although some breeds were used to capture prey only. Many of these breeds were hunted in packs, and the hunter either followed behind the dogs or waited for them to return to him after hunting. Group I sporting dogs include sighthounds, who rely on sight rather than scent to locate prey. These breeds, such as Salukis, Borzoi, Greyhounds, and Scottish Deerhounds, rely on a strong sensitivity to motion and a well-developed peripheral visual field to locate prey. Ancestral sighthound breeds, such as the Saluki, are thought to have originally been developed in Africa or Arabia, where speed, agility, independence, and tenacity were key to hunting gazelle in the wide-open deserts and savannahs of the region. Borzoi were developed to hunt wolves, fox, and hare in their native Russia, often in groups of 100 dogs or more. Greyhounds proved particularly useful in the British Isles for hunting rabbits, while their cousins, the Scottish Deerhounds, were used on deer and, for a considerable period of time, could only be owned by royalty of the rank "earl" or above. The independent nature of the hunting work, the highly developed chase reaction triggered by moving animals, and the killing instincts of these breeds set them apart in behavior and temperament from the breeds used to hunt in close cooperation with gun hunters.

Group II sporting dogs include the scenthounds, who rely mostly on their keen sense of smell to locate prey. Like the sighthounds, these dogs usually killed their prey once it was overtaken. Otterhounds, various breeds of coonhounds and foxhounds, Beagles, and the more recently developed Catahoula Leopard Dog, are a few of the breeds that fall in this group. Otterhounds were historically used to locate and kill nuisance otters in the rivers and streams of England. Coonhounds were developed from foxhound breeds and the two types of dogs share similar hunting strategies. Traditional raccoon hunts usually involved the work of one or more dogs to locate by scent and "tree" (corner) a raccoon. The hunter would then come to the pack and kill the raccoon or force it from its hiding place and allow the dogs to kill it. This is similar to a traditional fox hunt, where the hound pack, with hunters on horseback following them, would pursue the fox until it went to ground. A terrier would then be sent in to flush the fox out and the hound pack would kill the fox or continue the chase. Beagles were hunted in packs to locate hare, with hunters following on foot. Catahoula Leopard Dogs are used on a wide range of prey, including wild boar. Although most modern scenthound hunters no longer allow prey to be harmed, traditionally the scenthounds were used to kill prey and those instincts are still present in many of the scenthound breeds. Most breeds have a very strongly developed pack instinct, working in tightly-knit groups during the hunt, taking direction more from each other than from the hunters. They are extremely attracted to tracking activities, and, given their independent nature, display a unique personality different from that typically found in gun dog breeds.

Breeds that fall into Groups III and IV are those created to work under fairly close direction from hunters, and to forgo actually killing prey once it is located. Modern hunters using these breeds typically use guns to kill prey, which is then brought back by the dogs. These are the breeds most people think of when they think of a "sporting dog," and they are the focus of this training book.

Different breeds for different hunting needs

For centuries, ability trumped appearance when it came to choosing a dog to use for hunting. Even after the introduction of dog shows during the Victorian era, many sporting dog enthusiasts still placed a higher value on a dog's instinctual hunting ability than his outward appearance. Lee Rawdon admonished his readers in his 1883 *A History & Description of the Modern Dogs of Great Britain & Ireland (Sporting Division)*: "If you require a retriever for show purposes, buy one to answer your requirements; but, if such a dog is required for work, either by land or water or both, do not mind what colour or shape he may be, so long as his character for intelligence and tenderness is satisfactory." Many other breed historians and sportsmen writing at the time dog shows first started gaining popularity in the United Kingdom shared the same viewpoint. Over time, some of the more popular sporting breeds split into "field" lines, used strictly for hunting, and "show/companion" lines, developed to conform to written breed standards and to primarily serve as non-hunting companions. Many of the sporting dog pets people own today come from these "show/companion" lines. These dogs tend to be a little less driven to hunt than dogs from "field" lines and, in some breeds, vary considerably in appearance from their hunting counterparts. But they still share, to some degree, all the instincts to be hunting dogs their "field" relatives possess.

Under the categories Dalziel used to describe sporting dogs, the two groups he used for dogs that worked with gun hunters can be further split into five sub-groups, based on the specific manner these dogs worked in the field. Probably the best known of these sub-groups consists of the retriever breeds. According to the American Kennel Club, the Labrador Retriever has been the most popular breed of dog registered in the United States since 2002, and the Golden Retriever has bounced between the second and the fourth most popular breed registered during that same time period. In addition to these two well-known retriever breeds, the retriever family phrase also includes several other breeds, such as the Poodle and the less-common Curly-Coated Retriever.

Labrador Retrievers, like KoKo, are popular as family pets as well as hunting companions.

These breeds typically assist the hunter by finding and retrieving downed game on land as well as in water. British canine historian Lee Rawdon noted that British retriever breeds, including the Golden Retriever, were developed when British hunters found they needed quicker, bigger dogs than their setters, pointers, and spaniels to help find and retrieve game. The Chesapeake Bay Retriever is the American contribution to the retrievers of the world. Over the centuries, retrievers have been used to walk partridge, drive grouse, retrieve waterfowl, and retrieve dead and wounded upland birds and small mammals. In the United States, where the typical hunter could usually only afford a single dog to hunt with, the retriever became popular as an all-around hunting dog. The social nature of these dogs has been long recognized, even at a time when most hunting dogs never set foot inside their masters' homes. Lee advised late nineteenth-century sportsmen to "Let such an animal [a retriever] live in the house and be constituted a constant companion, and there is no knowing how sensible a creature he will prove when his services are required in the field."

Wesley and Boomer enjoy spending time with Izzy, even when family time involves playing dress up.

But there are other ways dogs help hunters find and kill game, based on the type of game being hunted and the cover hunted in. As explained by Desmond Morris in *Dogs: The Ultimate Dictionary of Over 1,000 Dog Breeds*: "The role of a flushing dog is to search the undergrowth in front of the guns, panic game birds from cover, wait for them to be shot and to drop and then, on command, locate the bodies and retrieve them to the hunters. In the era before sporting guns existed, the flushing dog's duty was much the same as it is today, except that when it drove the birds into the air they were killed by the hunter's hawks. An alternative method was to drive them into large nets, where they were trapped."

Spaniels are probably the best-known flushing breeds and the oldest described sporting dog developed to help hunters bring in game, both furred and feathered. Hunting spaniels are split into two broad groups—field spaniels (developed primarily for land hunting) and water spaniels (developed primarily for use in the water). Although field spaniels were developed to help the upland game hunter, they also work well as water retrievers, like their cousins the water spaniels.

Field Spaniel Caino fresh on the dock from a water retrieve.

References describing an Irish Water Spaniel-type dog have been found in Ireland dating to the 7th century. Written references by Chaucer in 1383 to "spaynels" and tapestries from that era depict spaniel-like dogs being used to help falcons hunt, as well as driving various types of game into nets before the widespread use of handheld guns changed the way hunters were able to capture game. Spaniels were also used to flush hare out for greyhound-coursing; after the spaniel located a hare and forced it from its warren, the greyhounds gave chase. As noted by Thomas Brown in *Biographical Sketches and Authentic Anecdotes of Dogs,* "differently from other dogs used in shooting, both the Springer and Cocker give tongue the moment they either smell or see game," helping hunters locate game in heavier cover. Even in the early 1800's, well before the concept of keeping a dog strictly for companionship became a reality, Dalziel noted: "The spaniel is no less a favourite as a companion and house dog, for which his watchfulness, sagacity, and fidelity, equally with his gentleness of manners and handsome appearance, eminently fit him."

Spaniels like Jack the Sussex Spaniel are handsome, happy hunting and family companions.

The third broad sub-group of sporting dogs used by gun hunters includes the setters. Setters were preferred by many hunters working in rugged, stony terrain under adverse weather conditions. Once referred to as "setting spaniels" or "crouching spaniels," it is likely these breeds had spaniel ancestors. The difference in hunting style between a setter and its modern spaniel cousin is that once a setter detects its quarry, it freezes in the direction of the prey and remains still until released by its handler, while the spaniel will move forward and purposefully flush the quarry. Although it may seem unnatural that a setter will "set," or freeze, in the presence of birds, Morris and others point out that wolves demonstrate this behavior instinctively. "Setting" in wolves occurs when the pack has surrounded its prey and is preparing for the final kill rush. Selective breeding has turned this natural canid behavior into one that helped the hunter. Prior to the appearance of practical hunting guns, setters worked to nets or falcons, similar to their spaniel relatives. With the advent of guns that could be carried and fired by a single person, setters were trained to the gun. Gordon Setters, Irish Setters, and English Setters were each developed to suit the unique environmental and quarry challenges of their local hunting areas.

English Setter Eva instinctively freezes when she catches the scent of a bird.

Pointers make up the fourth sub-group of sporting dogs and are famous (or infamous) for their stamina in the field and their slightly more independent personalities. Early forms of the pointer are thought to have been developed in Spain, Italy, and southern France, gradually making their way across Europe to the British Isles. A painting attributed to Titian (1477-1576) contains a likeness of a pointing dog, indicating they were known by the 15th century and quite possibly existed even earlier on the European continent, although they probably didn't arrive in Great Britain until the early 18th century. There, the early Pointers were found to be too heavy and slow to meet the needs of hunters, so refinements were made to the breed. The focus and intensity with which most pointer breeds worked sometimes made them less a companion to the hunter and more aloof than some of the other hunting breeds. Writing about the Pointer's physical characteristics and development in Hugh Dalziel's book *British Dogs*, nineteenth-century breed historian G. Thorpe-Bartram described the physical nature of Pointers:

> The pointer of to-day is an animal that has been produced by the most careful exercise of knowledge gained by keen observation, assisted by extensive breeding and sporting experience. He is a dog specially adapted to his work. He has been rendered capable of doing it with the greatest amount of ease and efficiency…. He is…capable of hunting a larger range of ground without becoming useless by excessive fatigue…. I do not think the pointer is such a companionable dog as the setter. He is 'all there' when at work…. He does not acquire so much affectionate amiability of character from his association with mankind as does the setter and other sporting dogs. Of course there are exceptions to every rule, and I know some few pointers that are remarkable

for their attachment and sagacity. Similar to the setters, the pointers rely on their keen sense of smell to locate birds, then freeze and "hold" their quarry until released to move forward. The characteristic position of one front leg lifted appears as if the dog is actually pointing at the quarry, waiting for the hunter to shoot. Arkwright describes the "point" as "… an artificial prolongation of the instinctive pause of a carnivorous animal on first becoming aware of the proximity of prey—a pause for the purpose of devising a stratagem…."

There are two basic types of modern pointer breeds—the "specialist" breeds who are used only to hunt and point, and the all-round breeds that can be used to hunt, point, and retrieve, often referred to as the HPR breeds. According to Morris in *Dogs: The Ultimate Dictionary of over 1,000 Dog Breeds,* the HPR breeds are the preferred breeds of choice for continental European hunters, and many North American hunters as well. The luxury of hunting with specialist breeds (one dog to locate and indicate the quarry, another to retrieve it) is one not many hunters can afford, so the sporting dog who can do it all is a practical helpmate for the modern hunter across the world. The versatile hunting breeds are those that can track, point, and retrieve equally well on land and water; the Weimaraner, Vizsla, Braque Francais, and Pudelpointers are just a few of the modern versatile hunting breeds.

Not all pointer breeds are aloof. Outlaw, a German Wirehaired Pointer, adores spending time with his family, whether it is in the field or at home.

The last sub-group of sporting dogs included in the breeds that are used by gun hunters are the "tolling," or decoy, dogs. Only two of these breeds are known to exist today. The Nova Scotia Duck Tolling Retriever and the Kookierhondje were developed to encourage waterfowl in closer to shore where they could be caught in traps (known as "kooi" in the Netherlands, where decoy dogs were once particularly popular) or shot with primitive firearms. These dogs were also used to retrieve downed birds from the water. A hunter using a decoy dog would toss a stick in the water for his dog to retrieve, and the bushy, wagging tail and erratic splashing activity of the dog would often catch the attention of the ducks, who would then swim in closer to investigate, making them easier to trap or shoot. Breed historians and naturalists alike are uncertain why these dogs are able to attract the attention of waterfowl, although fox are known to sometimes lure prey closer with similar behaviors. As firearms improved and hunters gained better range and accuracy with their weapons, the necessity of luring the birds in close to shore or going through the laborious process of trapping them decreased and these types of hunting dogs fell out of favor.

What about the oodles of Doodles and Poos?

The human desire to continue to alter dogs to suit our wants and needs for companion animals is alive and well today, as demonstrated by the abundance of "designer dogs" now available. Two of the most popular "designer lines" are the "Doodles" and the "Poos," dogs who are the product of a cross between a Poodle (a retriever breed) and some other breed of dog. Many of these crosses were originally done to try to reduce shedding in the subsequent generations, because Poodles shed very little compared to most other dogs. However, it is impossible to alter only those genes affecting a dog's coat characteristics when crossing two different dog breeds. Every genetic trait in both breeds can potentially be altered. In crosses involving Poodles and other sporting dogs, instincts aren't altered much because the two breeds used in the cross are already similar to one another in terms of behavioral traits. But crosses between Poodles and other dog breeds can result in unpredictable behavioral consequences that can be challenging for unprepared dog owners to handle.

Many of the more popular "Doodle" and "Poo" crosses involve a Poodle (usually a standard Poodle or miniature Poodle) and another sporting dog breed. These crosses include Labradoodles, Goldendoodles, and Cockapoos. Because the breeds used in these crosses have similar behavioral traits and working personalities, the offspring pretty much act like any other sporting dog, even though their outward appearances can vary widely from the two breeds used in the original cross.

However, other common breed crosses, such as Maltipoos, Schnoodles, Whoodles, Boodles, and Bernerdoodles, involve crossing a Poodle with another breed of dog who has very different behavioral instincts. The offspring of these crosses may no longer act at all like sporting dogs. The behavioral impact on the offspring of these crosses is much more significant and unpredictable. For example, crossing a Poodle, bred for generations to work closely with humans and to retrieve, not kill, dead or wounded animals, with a terrier breed, bred for generations to work independently from humans and outright kill other animals, can result in an interesting and potentially frustrating mix of instinctive behaviors in the offspring. This is often what happens in Schnoodles (Miniature Schnauzer and Poodle cross), Maltipoos (Maltese and Poodle cross),

Whoodles (Wheaten Terrier and Poodle cross) and many other crosses involving terrier breeds. The dog may exhibit instincts to retrieve as well as to kill, providing quite a training challenge to his owner. Crossing working or herding dogs, like Bernese Mountain Dogs or Border Collies, with Poodles can also lead to unpredictable instinctive behaviors that an owner will have to learn to deal with. This doesn't mean these crosses can't be wonderful companions who can be taught to behave appropriately just like any other dog, but the foundation instincts upon which the training is built may be more difficult to predict and work with when crosses involve two breeds originally created to perform very different types of work rather than two sporting breeds.

So what exactly is a sporting dog?

The management techniques and training exercises in this book can be used with any dog, but they were specifically selected for sporting dog breeds and crosses between two sporting breeds traditionally used to locate and/or retrieve game back to the hunter. The hunter is responsible for actually killing the game, which is usually some type of bird. These breeds may vary in how they behave while helping the hunter, but they all help find and bring back the game without killing it themselves. Breeds used to hunt and then kill game themselves, such as sighthounds, scenthounds, arboreal hounds, and big game dogs are not specifically addressed in this book. The instincts modified and intensified in hunting dogs who actually kill their quarry vary in many important ways from the instincts of those breeds who must work closely with hunters and restrain themselves from killing the game they find. Crosses between sporting dogs and terriers, working breeds, herding breeds, or toy dogs are also not included, because of the sometimes exceptional behavioral variations found in these crosses, as compared to crosses between sporting dog breeds. For a more complete list of these breeds used around the world, see the Appendix.

Chapter 2

Why Should I Care What Breed of

Dog I Own—Dogs are Dogs, Right?

The world was conquered through the understanding of dogs; the world exists through the understanding of dogs.

~ Friedrich Nietzsche
German philosopher

With so many different dog breeds and crosses available, *something* made each of us decide to share our hearts and homes with a sporting dog rather than any other type of dog. More often than not, the decision had absolutely nothing to do with needing the help of a hunting dog to put food on the family table. The size, appearance, and generally easy-going demeanor of the retrievers and most other sporting dogs give them the potential to be fantastic family pets, with proper training and management. But many people aren't prepared for the work it takes to help a sporting dog become a calm, happy household member. Understanding how sporting dogs differ from other breeds and the instinctual behaviors likely to develop in them can help tremendously with this process.

How instincts influence behavior

There are certain instincts that make sporting dogs behave like they do that we will never completely change. Some of these instincts are quite different from those that influence, for example, a Jack Russell Terrier's behavior. While the final behavior your dog learns may be the same, differences in instincts can lead to the need for slightly different approaches to training and rewarding appropriate retriever behavior, as compared to appropriate terrier behavior. Many dog owners willingly accept a one-size-fits-all training class approach, without regard to the unique needs of their particular dog. Fortunately, most reputable pet dog trainers have experience working with sporting breeds due to the sheer numbers of these breeds in the pet population, and therefore also in training classes. But is your dog being taught what he really needs to know become a calm, confident, enjoyable family companion in the most effective, efficient manner possible, while simultaneously being allowed some freedom to be what he is—a *sporting dog?* You don't need to buy a gun, field train your dog, and hunt with him to provide him a fulfilling sporting dog life; allowing him to carry things in his mouth, sniff after birds on a long walk with you, and be a part of your daily life will satisfy his innate need to be a hunting pack animal. Teaching him to exhibit self-control and work to earn the things he wants in life will help him become a calmer, confident, reliable companion, while at the same time giving him a job to do so he isn't bored. By appreciating and understanding your sporting dog's unique needs, you can provide him a satisfying life as a dog, enjoy him as a family member, and train him in a fun, effective way.

Vizslas Belle and Bode have been taught to have self-control when they see something interesting in the field, even when they are off-leash.

Although every dog is a unique individual, those developed to perform similar tasks tend to share more physical and behavioral traits in common with each other than with dogs developed to perform other tasks. As we already examined in Chapter 1, breeds developed to locate and/or retrieve game all perform the same basic task for the hunter, even though their specific hunting styles may vary; similarly, breeds developed to herd share certain characteristics which allow them to effectively herd livestock, and breeds developed to eradicate vermin share characteristics which facilitate killing other animals. Sporting dogs share more specific behavioral traits in common with each other than they do with herding dogs or terriers. That's why it isn't realistic or productive to expect a sporting dog to behave more like a herding dog or terrier than like another sporting dog and why training a sporting dog isn't exactly the same as training any other type of dog. Of course, any dog can be taught to sit, lie down, and walk politely on-leash, but his instinctual behaviors may very well influence the most effective way to train and reward those behaviors.

A tale of three breeds
Let's look at the role instincts can play in training by comparing three very different types of dogs. The Border Collie, the Jack Russell Terrier, and the Curly-Coated

Retriever are three British-refined dog breeds who, for generations, earned their keep by performing important work for their owners. They are all physically and mentally tough dogs, known for having fairly high pain tolerance and the ability to stay focused on a task for long periods of time. To varying degrees, each breed performs its work independently. The Border Collie was developed to move flocks of sheep over sometimes hazardous terrain with minimal direction or physical assistance from the shepherd. The instincts and independent working intelligence necessary for this type of work give Border Collies the reputation as being the "smartest" of all dog breeds (we'll come back to this point in a moment).

Gabriel ready to herd.

The Jack Russell Terrier was developed for use during fox hunts to force fox who found underground refuge from the hound pack back to the surface, so the hunt could continue. Famous for their tenacity and single-minded determinedness to complete this task, these terriers were also highly valued by those in need of general vermin exterminators. Cleverness is a key characteristic of the breed.

Lizzie B. can't wait to be released to begin hunting at an AKC earthdog test.

The Curly-Coated Retriever was developed to locate and retrieve shot wildfowl, often from extremely frigid waters. They were known as the premier "meat dog" for game-keepers and poachers alike due to their intelligence, tenacity and ability to locate downed birds by scent. The American Kennel Club breed standard refers to Curlys as being "wickedly smart."

Jet proudly displays a day's work in the field.

Looking at the jobs performed by each of these three breeds, the work for which they were bred clearly required dogs who exhibited intelligence, physical strength, courage, independence, and endurance. These general behavioral attributes create broad similarities between these three breeds. But the job each breed performed also required very specific skills. The process of selective breeding insured that some basic canine instincts were preserved or even intensified, while at the same time others were diminished, resulting in the unique physical appearance, temperament, and innate behavioral skills now present in each breed. Although these three breeds have many characteristics in common, they also differ in many significant ways which are important to take into consideration when training.

The primary behavior chain that humans altered to develop dogs which could perform the tasks done by these three breeds is the basic predatory behavior chain dogs inherited from their wild canid ancestors. To be a successful hunter, a predator must carry out a series of behaviors: namely, eye-stalk-chase-grab-shake-kill-eat-guard carcass remains. For example, a wolf first locates his prey by using his eyesight, sense of smell, and hearing. Once located, the wolf will watch and then start slowly stalking the prey. When the prey begins to run, the wolf chases; when larger prey animals are involved, the chase is often a shared activity between members of the pack. The kill is usually accomplished by a bite to the neck, followed by a series of violent shakes that breaks the prey's spine or neck. Then the feast can begin. The carcass remnants are sometimes guarded until the entire animal is consumed. This is the basic behavior chain which was modified in different ways to create herding dogs, terriers, and sporting dogs.

Shepherds are able to use dogs to herd livestock because prey animals instinctively avoid predators, while simultaneously trying to maintain the integrity of the flock or herd. From a sheep's point of view, a herding dog is simply a wolf in dog's clothing. From the herding dog's point of view, a sheep is merely a mutton-meal-on-the-hoof. Herding is an elaborate dance between predator (dog) and prey (sheep) that has been choreographed by carefully altering the basic predatory behavior chain in herding dog breeds. Through generations of selective breeding, Border Collies were developed to have extremely strong eye, stalk, and chase behaviors, but the grab-shake-kill-eat-guard portions of the predatory behavior chain were weakened. It is pointless to have a herding dog that kills the very animals he is supposed to be herding. Although the shepherd may give his Border Collie directions, an independent nature and exceptional problem-solving skills are genetically hard-wired into Border Collies to help them appropriately interact with livestock. All of these instinctual alterations combine to form the foundation of the aloof, controlling "herding personality" that is common in most Border Collies. As a result of these instincts, most Border Collies must be taught to resist the urge to herd anything that moves (including people) and to take direction from their owners, rather than take charge themselves. Border Collies tend to be indifferent or aloof to people they don't know, often preferring work to play.

From a sheep's point of view, Gabriel resembles a black-and-white wolf.

Working terrier breeds were originally developed to locate and harass or kill some type of vermin, ranging in size from mice to badgers and otters. Only the last two steps in the predatory behavior chain—namely, eating and guarding—have been significantly altered in these breeds. Working terriers had to locate, stalk, chase, grab, shake, and harass or kill vermin, then leave the prey alone once it died (or quit moving). Terriers were bred to move quickly, bite decisively and lethally, and shake prey to kill quickly and efficiently; those dogs which moved slowly or hesitated when going for the kill were often hurt or killed themselves. "Giving voice" (barking) was a trait specifically enhanced in terriers used to work quarry underground. Although outright aggression toward other dogs was never desired, most early terriers worked alone and didn't necessarily need to get along with other dogs to do their daily work.

This slightly truncated predatory behavior chain present in all working terrier breeds is particularly well-preserved in Jack Russell Terriers. The hard-wired behaviors common in the Jack Russell Terrier often result in dogs who are quite vocal when excited, willing to chase, harass, and quite possibly kill anything that moves like prey without hesitation (including cats, birds, vacuum sweepers, and squeaky toys), and to "bite first, ask questions later" when overstimulated. Jacks are notorious for not getting along particularly well with other dogs, even dogs they've lived with all their lives. They are independent thinkers and actors. Combined with intrinsically high energy levels and tenacity, these hard-wired traits can be very problematic if they aren't channeled into more appropriate behaviors. These instincts combine to produce the feisty, tenacious, vocal "terrier personality" displayed by many terriers. These dogs must often be taught to work cooperatively with their owners, tolerate the presence of other dogs, and resist the urge to chase and grab anything that moves too quickly.

The only thing stopping Glitch from going underground to explore an animal's den is his leash.

Using a dog to help a hunter locate and retrieve game required slightly different manipulations of the predatory behavior chain than those used to develop herding or terrier breeds. The predatory instincts to stalk-grab-shake-kill-eat-guard were modified in the Curly-Coated Retriever to produce a dog which, with proper training, would eye game (usually as it falls from the sky after being shot), stalk and grab it, and then fetch the game back to his handler without damaging or eating it. A retriever must grasp birds firmly but gently to return them to the hunter intact, so a "soft mouth" is required; the instinct to shake-kill-eat-guard has been greatly diminished. Retrievers must also be quiet when working, since unnecessary barking in the field could scare game beyond firing range. Many hunters work more than one dog a time when hunting and may hunt out of small blinds or boats, so retrievers must be comfortable spending long periods of time in close proximity to other dogs and working together with them. The behaviors genetically hard-wired in a Curly-Coated Retriever combine to form the foundation of the hard-working, willing-to-please "retriever personality" that makes retriever breeds so popular as family pets. These instincts result in dogs who readily accept direction from people ("biddability") and will tolerate a certain amount of repetitive training better than some other breeds because of their strong desire to work together with their owners. They usually must be taught self-control to properly direct their enthusiasm for interacting with people.

Curly-Coated Retriever Eli is a useful hunting companion, both in and out of the water.

By manipulating the basic canid predatory behavior chain in three different ways over generations of selective breeding, three very different breeds were created to help man perform three very different types of tasks. These differences and traits are what make each breed unique and they still exist in our present-day dogs, even though most Border Collies no longer herd sheep, most Jack Russell Terriers no longer go to ground after fox or kill rats, and most Curly-Coated Retrievers no longer retrieve game. These traits are also why a sporting dog doesn't act exactly the same as a herding dog or terrier (or any other type of dog, for that matter). And these traits are why you can never train your sporting dog to act exactly like the Border Collie next door or the Jack Russell Terrier you owned as a child. The only way to have a dog who behaves just like a Border Collie is to have a Border Collie in the first place. Although every dog has a unique personality, the odds are much more in your favor that a sporting dog will behave more like another dog of the same breed than like a Border Collie. Even though all dogs can be taught basic manners and can adapt to living in our modern world, there will always be behavioral and personality differences that no amount of training can change. Accepting and understanding the dog you see at the end of your leash and the behaviors he is likely to exhibit without any training will help you train him to be the best *sporting dog* companion he can be.

Although Barnum and Jinx share many instincts, they will always be very different types of dogs at heart.

The power of sporting dog-centric training

Understanding breed instincts allows us to better understand what "normal" behavior is for sporting dogs. *But normal behavior is not necessarily the same as acceptable behavior.* When a dog becomes overstimulated or stressed, his behaviors will likely reflect his breed instincts. For example, when a sporting dog sees a bird, his normal instinctual urge may be to set, point and/or grab the bird, depending on his breed. He may bark or he may remain silent; he may quiver with excitement or frantically chase after the bird. This is all perfectly normal behavior for a sporting dog who has not been taught how to properly react around birds, even though it isn't necessarily behavior you want your dog to engage in on a regular basis. Sporting dogs that seemingly lose their minds at the mere sight or scent of birds are not stupid, stubborn, or out of control—they are normal sporting dogs engaging in normal, instinctual sporting dog behavior. It is up to us to teach them how to behave differently if that is what we expect them to do.

The power of sporting dog-centric training lies in understanding the very essence of the sporting dogs we've brought into our homes and appreciating our sporting dogs for what they are, rather than trying to make them into something they aren't. This doesn't mean that we should use the fact that they are sporting dogs to excuse, justify, or accept unsafe or inappropriate behaviors. Nor is owning a sporting dog a free pass to avoid training him to be a well-behaved companion or a reason to set limits on what he can achieve. But understanding sporting dog instincts is the key to developing a proactive, appropriate, and realistic training plan for reaching any goal we set for ourselves and our dogs. Working *with* the "sportiness" in our dogs, instead of against it, will make everyone much happier and allow us to unleash the full potential of our sporting dogs!

By working with, instead of against the sporting instincts Titus has, his owners will help him become the best Weimaraner he can be, as well as a welcome addition to the family.

Chapter 3

What is Typical Sporting Dog

Behavior?

Endurance n. the ability to withstand hardship or adversity; especially: the ability to sustain a prolonged stressful effort or activity

Joie de vivre n. Fr. keen or buoyant enjoyment of life

Distractibility n. to draw or direct (as one's attention) to a different object or in different directions at the same time

~ Merriam-Webster online dictionary

It is important to understand that a dog's personality and behavior are influenced not only by genetic predisposition, but also by environmental factors and unique individual experiences. However, there are several characteristics sporting dogs tend to share in common. A sporting dog may not exhibit all these traits all the time—in fact, your dog might not show some of these behaviors at all. The specific behaviors you will see from your dog depend on a number of factors, including his genetic makeup, experiences he had before you even brought him home, all the experiences and training you've done (or not done) with him after you brought him home, and his own unique personality. Dogs are thinking, feeling individuals, so no one can ever say with 100% certainty how a particular dog will behave based strictly on what is considered "normal" sporting dog behavior. But it's a safe bet that your dog has shown you at least one of these traits at some point in his life. We've already explored the ways a sporting dog is different from any other type of dog, so now let's look at some of the behavioral traits these breeds share with each other.

High energy levels and physical endurance

Writing in 1840, John Colquhoun, in *The Moor and the Loch*, offers his expertise on selecting hunting dogs. In his opinion, "the most necessary qualifications of a dog are travel, lastiness, and nose." In other words, hunters need dogs with physical and mental endurance who can locate game readily. These dogs had to be able to hunt all day, day after day if necessary, to help a hunter put meat on the table for his family. Hunting for sport and pleasure didn't come within the reach of the average person until well into the late 1800's, after the Industrial Revolution, urbanization, and changes in work life left more people with the time and money to pursue hunting more casually. Even then, sporting dogs were expected to be able to hunt as long and as often as their owners were able to hunt. Physical and mental stamina were vital to the early sporting dogs, and those key traits still exist in our sporting dogs today, even though the vast majority of them will never be used to hunt. Miles of rough terrain, harsh weather conditions, and taxing physical labor were just a few of the challenges that faced our dogs' ancestors. The dogs who could successfully meet those hardships were the ones most likely to pass their genes down to future generations and, as a result, our dogs still have the physical capacity to deal with these situations (with proper training and physical conditioning, of course). Very few of our modern sporting dog companions come close to getting the amount of physical exercise they need to be physically fit and mentally comfortable. Pent up energy tends to express itself in inappropriate ways, such as jumping, barking, and digging. Successful sporting dog owners who find ways to decrease these high energy levels have a head start on reducing behavioral problems and making their dogs' training much easier.

Field Spaniel Nova greatly benefits from regular vigorous exercise both on land and in the water.

Intelligence

Two common beliefs among many first-time sporting dog owners are: 1) sporting dogs are so smart they just "know" how to behave without any training; and 2) when the dogs don't behave appropriately, it is because they are stubborn or seeking revenge for some imagined wrong. But neither of these beliefs are true. Although sporting dogs are known for their keen intelligence, they are born knowing only how to be *dogs*, with absolutely no understanding of what the rules are for dogs living in a human world. Fortunately for sporting dog owners, these breeds are also known to be easy for most people to train as a result of their intelligence, but training is a must if you are to keep one step ahead of your sporting dog and help him become an enjoyable family companion.

In his book *The Intelligence of Dogs*, researcher Stanley Coren divides canine intelligence into several categories, including working/obedience intelligence, instinctive intelligence, and adaptive intelligence. Working/obedience intelligence measures how well a dog will learn to perform commands and act under the direction of humans. This is the most common measure of canine "intelligence" because this is the type of intelligence that is most desirable in a pet. In most cases, the average dog owner simply wants a well-behaved dog who doesn't take much effort to train and is willing to please. Competitive obedience trials measure this type of intelligence. Sporting dogs usually excel in this particular measure of intelligence.

Keagan eagerly works with Karen to perfect precision heeling and other obedience exercises.

Instinctive intelligence is also strong in most sporting dogs, especially those dogs who come from field lines which are still used to hunt. This type of intelligence focuses on the genetically determined behavioral predispositions which dogs inherit. In sporting dogs, these would include things such as "birdiness," pointing, setting, retrieving, and other typical sporting dog behaviors and inclinations. However, these behaviors require refinement through training to be truly useful to the hunter.

Poppy would naturally retrieve as a puppy, but she needed more training to become a reliable retrieving dog as an adult.

So what does all this mean for a sporting dog owner? It means a sporting dog is generally a very willing and eager learner, but you will have to take responsibility for teaching him how to behave appropriately, taking into account his instincts. If you are consistent and persistent, your sporting dog will rival any other dog as a phenomenal family pet and well-trained companion.

Lack of self-control (AKA excessive *joie de vivre*)

Sporting dogs are a gregarious lot; life is good, and they are more than happy to remind everyone of that. Jumping on people, constantly shadowing and pestering people for attention, and a general lack of self-control when excited are all related to the sporting dog *joie de vivre*. Without consistent, persistent training, these behaviors can become quite problematic. Many people who have small children choose a sporting dog as a family pet because these breeds are generally known to be good with kids. However, living in families with small children often exacerbates this lack of self-control in dogs. Kids will be kids, running, laughing, yelling and, in general, behaving in ways that invite an already exuberant sporting dog to get even more wound up and excited.

Some sporting dogs also exhibit a dangerous lack of self-control when it comes to interacting with other dogs. They enjoy the company of other dogs and get so excited that they behave in ways that are rude and unacceptable. Rushing up to another dog, insisting on physical interaction, and moving too fast are all common sporting dog social *faux pas* that can create dangerous situations, including fights. It is just as rude, from a canine perspective, to run up on another dog in a senseless, frenetic whirlwind of happy activity as it is to stand and growl at another dog who is not even making eye contact. Either behavior can cause fear and an understandable outburst from a dog who doesn't want his space invaded in this way. This is a big problem for many sporting dog owners, and we will look at this behavior in more detail in Chapter 4.

The happy-go-lucky antics Tuuri displays as a puppy may not be appropriate when he becomes an adult.

Close bonding with family members

A strong desire to work together with his owner is a critical trait for any successful sporting dog. A hunter asks his dog to do physically demanding work and give up a potential meal without hesitation every time he shoots a bird and sends his dog out to retrieve it. This strong desire to work with people is one reason many sporting dog breeds are such popular pet choices. But this close bonding has its down side—sporting dogs tend to want to be with their people 25/8/366. Separation from people for extended periods of time can sometimes cause separation anxiety and other behavioral problems. The desire to work together with their owners can cause these dogs to constantly pester and shadow family members, in an attempt to get interaction. People with lifestyles that involve extended periods of time away from home each day, or people that want dogs that are not so socially needy, often struggle with this aspect of sporting dog behavior.

Bode enjoys being with Shay and the rest of her family no matter what they are doing.

"Distractibility"

"Distractibility" is an element of instinctive intelligence that sporting dogs may exhibit. To hunt requires a dog to pay attention to things on the ground as well as in the sky. Sights as well as smells become very important to sporting dogs once they get in "bird mode." Instincts kick in and they tend to pay less attention to their owners and more attention to that little voice inside them telling them to find that bird. This focus and tenacity when it comes to tasks is a useful sporting dog trait if it is focused in the proper direction or a nightmare if it isn't focused properly.

"Oral" lifestyle

Sporting dogs live a very "oral" life compared to most other types of dogs. Finding, picking up, and carrying items is the *raison d'être* for most sporting dogs, especially retrievers. When a sporting dog is happy or excited, he likes to carry something in his mouth. When he is uncertain about what to do, he often defaults to putting something in his mouth. If he needs to calm down, he puts something in his mouth. It doesn't matter to him if it is the glove off your hand or your hand itself, holding something in his mouth is an instinctive and comforting activity for most sporting dogs. So is it any wonder why many owners find themselves constantly taking things out of their dogs' mouths, especially when the dogs are young? This trait is very useful when channeled in an appropriate direction, but very irritating when it is out of control. Many new sporting dog owners are shocked at the amount of destruction an untrained, under-exercised, unmanaged sporting dog can do in a relatively short amount of time.

Another unfortunate consequence of this "oral" life is the uncanny ability some sporting dogs seem to have to play with, chew on, and swallow the most odd, disgusting, and sometimes life-threatening, things imaginable. In a moment of boredom, a sporting dog may start to play with pieces of mulch in the flowerbed and end up eating them. In a moment of excitement, something being carried can quickly become something swallowed. And because many sporting dogs, Labs and Goldens in particular, are known to be pretty indiscriminate when it comes to food, many have the habit of swallowing anything remotely resembling a legitimate food item without bothering to smell or lick it to see if it is actually edible first. Since sporting dogs are bred to carry things in their mouths, the odds are pretty good they will eventually swallow something that wasn't meant to be swallowed. And just because a dog can swallow something far enough down that you can't see it when you look in his mouth doesn't mean he can't still choke on it or that the item will pass safely through his intestinal tract. Intestinal blockage can be fatal; always err on the side of caution if you see your dog swallow something he shouldn't and immediately call your veterinarian for advice. And even if you don't see him swallow anything out of the ordinary, if your chow hound suddenly starts to refuse his food, vomits, stops having bowel movements, or just seems "off," immediately contact your veterinarian for a diagnosis and treatment. If your dog suffers an intestinal blockage, it is critical to get him veterinary help as quickly as possible.

The only thing Flat-Coated Retrievers Misty, Susie, and Denzel enjoy more than retrieving a bumper is retrieving a bumper together!

Pulling it all together

Now that we've examined several of the common sporting dog behaviors in the context of the work sporting dogs were historically bred to do, it is easier to understand why our sporting dogs behave as they do. These behaviors don't happen because our sporting dogs are stubborn or spiteful. They happen because our sporting dogs are just that—sporting dogs. We need to learn how to manage our sporting dogs proactively to prevent inappropriate behaviors from happening in the first place and what to teach our sporting dogs so they can conform to the basic rules of our human world, keeping in mind these rules are often in direct conflict with the basic rules of the canine world. We have to be patient, persistent, consistent, and realistic with our expectations and understand that the instincts in every sporting dog can be controlled, but never completely eliminated. We should respect and enjoy that wonderful bundle of sporting dog instincts we brought into our home. When we accept sporting dogs for what they are, training will become a positive, productive journey we take together rather than a regimen we inflict on our dogs and ourselves.

Chapter 4

Socialization, Puppy Classes, and a Word about Dog Parks

A puppy is but a dog, plus high spirits, and minus common sense.

~ Agnes Repplier
American essayist

Many dog owners buy an eight-week-old puppy, then wait until the dog is six months or older to start exposing him to the world beyond his backyard or enroll him in a puppy training class. They don't realize proper socialization and early training are two irreplaceable ingredients in the recipe for a happy, confident, socially skilled adult sporting dog. Let's look at what you can do when your sporting dog is a puppy to help insure that you maximize your chances of having a dog you can live with as he matures.

Socialization

When most dog owners think about socializing their puppies, they think about taking them to a dog park or doggie daycare to play with other puppies. Unfortunately, there's much more involved in properly socializing your puppy. Socialization is *not* merely play, although appropriate play is an important part of socialization. In *The Dog Vinci Code*, John Rogerson, a well-known British canine behaviorist, defines socialization as learning how to interact appropriately with people, other dogs, and the environment. Socialization involves exposing your puppy to as many things as possible during the first sixteen weeks of his life, before he develops fear of new things. Your puppy needs to learn how to appropriately interact with other dogs, how to accept physical confinement and brief periods of isolation, how to ride in the car, how to accept being handled by you and other people, how to cope with unique environmental conditions where you live (such as neighborhood noises, sights, and smells), and how to deal with unique family situations (such as babies, the elderly, medical equipment, and pets of other species). Every socialization experience should be short, pleasant, and puppy-appropriate, but the experiences should reflect the environment you expect your adult sporting dog to live in and any work you might want him to do later in life. Investing in the time and effort it takes to properly socialize your sporting dog puppy will result in huge benefits that will last your dog's entire lifetime.

These Sussex Spaniel puppies are exposed to a variety of environmental stimuli even before their eyes are open.

A dog's behavior is influenced by both his genetic makeup and the environment he lives in (i.e., the intentional and unintentional socialization experiences and training he receives). Puppy brains grow just like all the other parts of their bodies; without proper environmental stimulation during the brain's growth period, the brain won't develop to its full potential and those instinctive behaviors may not ever be fully expressed. The stimulation you give your young sporting dog should either enhance the genetic instincts you want to increase in your dog or counteract the instincts you want to decrease in his behavior. For example, we have already considered how a sporting dog's genetic inheritance determines his general behavioral traits. Most popular sporting dog breeds are born with a strong predisposition to carry objects in their mouths. That is part of what makes them useful as hunting companions. But a sporting dog who is never allowed to carry or hold things in his mouth, especially while he is a young dog, may never fully develop that retrieving instinct he carries around in his genes. He still has the capacity to act on his instincts, but his environmental experiences and related brain development may diminish his natural desire to retrieve, as compared to a sporting dog who was provided the opportunity to explore, hold, and carry various things in his mouth as a puppy.

Virginia carefully exposes her English Springer Spaniel puppy to swimming, retrieving, different breeds of adult dogs, and many other things Lainie will need to cope with later in life as a hunting dog and family companion.

The same rules apply to teaching your puppy proper canine social skills. Dogs have the instinctive ability to express themselves in ways that other dogs understand. However, if a dog is not given the opportunity to practice and refine these communication skills during the first sixteen weeks of his life, his fluency will be greatly diminished and he may have problems throughout his life being socially appropriate with other dogs. He needs to be exposed to dogs of both sexes, different physical appearances (color, size, shape, coat length, head shape), different ages, and different predispositions to playing with puppies. It is vital your puppy interacts with dogs who will tell him to bug off (in a socially appropriate way, of course) so he learns that not every dog wants to play and also how to stop potential conflicts from escalating. If your sporting dog grows up only interacting with other puppies or adult dogs who tolerate his immature play style, he might not act appropriately the first time he encounters a dog who wants to be left alone. Although it is very important that your sporting dog learns how to interact with the dogs he lives with, his communication skills will be limited by the degree of fluency his housemates have in canine communication if those are the only dogs he interacts with as a puppy.

Play is another key part of socialization. Puppy play is Mother Nature's way of teaching puppies how to be predators (eye, stalk, chase, and grab skills are all part of typical puppy play) and how to communicate with one another (bite inhibition, social deference, and other skills also develop through play). Once puppies are four to six months old, these lessons are pretty much learned (or not learned, if the puppy wasn't adequately socialized) and the desire to play naturally diminishes. This is not to say that older puppies and adult dogs don't still "play" with other dogs, but the nature and frequency of that play changes. Just as adult humans usually don't "play" with friends in the same way they used to play together as kindergartners, adult dogs generally engage in different types of play as adults than they did as puppies. The all-out extended chase, tumble, and chew games puppies play with each other usually settle down to more casual shared environmental exploration and simply being "together." A well-socialized adult dog expects other adult dogs to behave like what they are— adults. Unfortunately, far too many sporting dogs tend to act like puppies their entire lives, due to their social nature and often a lack of proper puppy socialization, and this can cause dangerous encounters with other adult dogs.

Sporting dogs generally get along with other dogs fairly well. As they gained popularity as family pets, the human desire to have a dog who gets along with other dogs and is easy to assimilate into the average urban living situation led to a gradual selection for more juvenile, or "neotonized," play behaviors in some sporting breeds, especially Goldens and Labs. As a result, many doggie daycares are full of adult retrievers who act like puppies around other adult dogs. In effect, these dogs are big, furry, social nerds who stand a little too close, bark a little too loud and too long, and often irritate the living daylights out of other adult dogs by whining, licking, groveling, and being in a state of constant, meaningless motion. This tendency is even more evident in dogs who never encountered another dog who told them to calm down during the critical socialization period.

While it may seem that there is no harm done by an adult dog who acts like a puppy, the truth is, this inappropriate behavior is just as potentially dangerous as the behaviors exhibited by an adult dog who actively tries to keep other dogs away. Both forms of behavior are inappropriate in most situations and can trigger defensive behaviors in other, well-socialized dogs. If an out-of-control sporting dog nerd doesn't know how to read another dog's signals to calm down, back off, and "grow up," an escalation of behaviors can occur and a fight can break out. This is not because the nerd wanted to start a fight or because the other dog is "vicious" or "aggressive," but because the nerd didn't back off when told to by the other dog. "No" means "no," even in canine language, and not every adult dog wants to be mauled to death with love by another dog. The sweet, loving dog who is "just trying to be friendly" may very well be the one who accidently starts a fight.

Interactions with as many different types of socially appropriate adult dogs as possible, and consistent enforcement of bite inhibition when interacting with people are also critical to proper social development. Playing with other puppies is good, but puppy play alone is not adequate for socializing your puppy to other dogs. Puppies need to have their instinctive communication skills refined under the guidance of adult dogs who are already fluent in the language. If your puppy only plays with puppies who tolerate his over-exuberant play style, your puppy will grow up thinking such frenetic behavior is appropriate, and chances are very good he will eventually get into trouble when he finally meets up with a dog who won't tolerate such behaviors from an adult dog.

Unfortunately, an intense period of fear development partially overlaps the optimal period of learning many critical adult behaviors. So it is important to protect your puppy from traumatic experiences while still providing him with positive ones.

Throwing him into a mob scene with a pack of strange dogs at the dog park is *not* a good idea. Chances are good that your puppy will be scared by such an experience and this can greatly impair his social skill development. He might think that any time he meets a strange dog, he is going to be hurt. It is far safer to have your young puppy interact with dogs of known temperament or with a few other dogs under the supervision of a trainer in a controlled environment, such as training class, than to toss him out to fend for himself in the dog park. Although this requires more effort on your part, remember that you are creating a behavioral foundation that will last your dog's entire life.

Puppy classes

The most important training class you will ever select for your sporting dog is his early puppy class. Ideally, the puppy class you choose will place a lot of emphasis on having puppies learn to interact with other dogs outside their home "pack" during the optimal development stage for learning social skills. While you will want your puppy to learn skills in the more formal training segment of the class (most classes introduce sit, down, come, and walk on-leash), make sure he will also get the opportunity to learn from playtime experiences in class, which should include interaction with other puppies, adult dogs, unique environmental stimuli, and a variety of people (usually the other owners in the class) in a controlled, supervised setting.

Unfortunately, not all classes are created equal. Take the time to call around and inter-view several training facilities if you are fortunate enough to have access to multiple classes in your area. Below is a list of questions to help you interview prospective trainers when selecting your early puppy class.

How are puppies introduced to each other when they start class? Puppies should be introduced to each other in a controlled manner. This is particularly important with sporting dog puppies who may need to learn self-control in social situations. Puppies should be released one or two at a time to greet each other so there is a trickle of greetings rather than a flood. Even if all the puppies have played peacefully together before, allowing a puppy to be swamped by his "friends" at the entrance to the play area can cause problems. The more exciting the gate to the play group area is, the more excited your puppy will get anticipating his play time. If you allow him to crazily pull to the play group and release him to run full speed into the area, you are teaching him to be a social nerd as an adult. While it is normal for puppies to enjoy and be excited about playtime, the calmer you keep the initial entrance into the group, the more self-control your puppy will learn and the calmer he will be when meeting his playmates. He will then have time to actually see, interpret, and react to the signals the others in the group are giving him, preparing him for a lifetime of social appropriateness.

How are puppies divided up for playtime? Ideally, the class you choose has enough physical space and staff to provide for more than one play group if the personalities and play styles of the puppies in class require that type of division. Play group forma-tion should be based more on play style and age than physical size. Be aware that groups will change as puppies mature and their play styles and personalities naturally change. A play group that did well when all the puppies were three months old might fall apart when they are four months old, or with the introduction of new puppy to the group. A slow, mellow St. Bernard puppy might make the perfect play companion for a shy Cocker pup—the differences in size are balanced by the differences in play style and the ability of the smaller puppy to outmaneuver the larger one, if necessary. On the other hand, a physically tough young Lab puppy might not be a good play companion for a Yorkshire Terrier puppy since the Lab's play style might be too rough for the Yorkie and could result in unintended physical injury. While the Lab, with enough time and experiences, can and should learn to exhibit bite inhibition and slow down play with smaller, "softer" dogs, the likelihood that an active Lab puppy will naturally override his instincts to play all out with other dogs is fairly low, unless he is taught this lesson appropriately by an older puppy or adult dog. You never want your sporting dog to practice being a bully or a nerd who won't take no for an answer. If he is only playing with other puppies and is allowed to interact in inappropriate ways, that is *exactly* what he is learning. This is why having adult dogs in the play group is so important. We don't have kindergartners teaching other kindergartners in our schools how to behave without the supervision of an adult teacher, so why would we rely solely on puppies teaching other puppies how to behave in dog school without the supervision of an adult dog?

Are socially-appropriate adult dogs in the play group as well? This is probably the most important question of all for sporting dog owners to ask about play groups. One of the best ways for puppies to learn how to behave appropriately around other dogs is to have them interact with a socially-appropriate adult dog who isn't impressed by puppy antics. This isn't an adult dog who wants to kill every puppy he sees, but an adult dog who will interact with puppies to some degree but will also draw appropriate behavioral boundaries for puppies and correct them consistently and effectively if they cross those boundaries. Properly socialized adult dogs can administer such a correction in a way that is quick, effective, and appropriate for the severity of the puppy's social transgression. You can see this type of schooling in action if you have ever watched a bitch interact with her puppies. She is patient, but only to a certain point. Her patience with her puppies' behavior is inversely proportional to the age of the puppies; the older the puppies, the less craziness the bitch will tolerate from them. If your puppy only ever plays with other puppies who don't tell him "no" on occasion, he won't learn how to read stop signals from other dogs and he can end up being an adult social nerd.

Are other owners involved in playtime? It is a good experience for your sporting dog pup to meet as many people as possible, especially during the first four or five months of his life. But keep in mind that other well-intentioned people can teach your puppy bad habits, sometimes right before your eyes! For example, dog lovers often say "It's OK—I don't mind if your puppy jumps up on me. I love dogs!" It's nice to know that someone doesn't mind being physically assaulted by your puppy, but keep in mind that this same dog lover is teaching your dog to act rudely whenever he meets someone new! If owners are in the play group, they should be encouraged to gently turn away and ignore any puppy that jumps up on them for attention. Puppies also shouldn't be allowed to congregate under anyone's legs, especially their owner's legs. Puppies who hide behind their owners can become quite snarky to other puppies, because they feel safer around their owners; this can cause unnecessary and inappropriate squabbles to break out. There is also less room for a puppy to physically maneuver if he is between your feet, so it becomes harder for him to flee a situation if necessary. Owners should be encouraged to stand and move around during playtime to prevent this from happening. Every interaction your puppy has with *anyone* or *anything* is a learning experience for him, so be sure he is learning what *you* want him to learn!

How are children handled during playtime? Parents often bring young children to training classes, which can also cause training problems if the children are allowed to run and play in play group along with the puppies. Again, it is important that your puppy meets young children, but you should be prepared to help your puppy maintain self-control around them. You never want your puppy to chase and possibly nip a person or child, even in play. If kids are running freely in play group, it is far better to err on the side of caution and not put your puppy in the group than risk him getting overly excited and nipping a child.

Does the instructor supervise playtime? Does he/she explain what is going on and when to intervene vs. when to leave the puppies alone? If the instructor or another concerned owner consistently intervenes in an excited or forceful way every time a squabble breaks out between puppies, he might inadvertently trigger a fight, doing more harm than good. Once a fight is underway, grabbing and pulling dogs away from each other haphazardly can cause even more harm to the puppies and may get people bit as well. So it is critical that your instructor understands canine body language and has experience with the various play postures and vocalizations that are common and normal for puppies when they play, so that he can read the group and intervene before any puppy gets too aroused. In general, if puppies are having a tussle, gently walking through the group or calling the puppies away with a toy or treat can prevent escalation. And if the puppy that was on the bottom of the pile (i.e., the one that appears to be getting "picked on") runs right back to the other puppies after you've gently separated them, then you can allow that group to continue to play, even if the play looks rough or the vocalizations sound awful. You gave the puppy a chance to run away or play with other puppies, but instead he chose to go back to the group that you just broke up; he is comfortable with the dynamics and understands what the other puppies are telling him. Of course, you should continue to watch any fast-paced play to be sure the puppies don't get over-aroused, but you don't need to keep the puppies separate if nothing escalates. However, if the puppy on the bottom flees the group when you break them up, then the instructor needs to take steps to keep that puppy from being scared and the other puppies from bullying him.

Is there separate physical "time out" space for overly-aroused puppies? Choosing a class in which the instructor uses time-outs to remove an overly aroused puppy temporarily from the group typically creates the best opportunity for your sporting dog to learn self-control in social situations. Arousal indicates a heightened emotional state; adrenaline is starting to flow and your sporting dog is now dancing on the edge of a behavioral knife. If the arousal doesn't escalate, he will be able to maintain some semblance of self-control and behave appropriately toward other puppies. That is a good thing and it is what you want your sporting dog to learn. However, if the arousal escalates, he will lose self-control and a fight may break out even though your puppy isn't being aggressive toward the other puppies. He may just be "too much," and if he can't calm himself down when another puppy says "Stop!" the other puppy may lash out understandably in self-defense. Either way, a fight is a fight and neither puppy learns anything positive from such an encounter. Either you or the instructor should immediately interrupt the behavior and remove your puppy from the situation when he starts to get too excited to control himself, long before he reaches the point of no return. Interrupting calmly and early will help avoid escalations. Standing in the group restraining your puppy or actually holding him in your arms if he is small enough will only excite him more; he won't understand he is being held because he is too excited. He will just get even more excited while you restrain him because he is still watching the other puppies playing and he wants to rejoin them. There should be access to a quiet space in the facility or the ability to go outside until play time is over to successfully handle these types of situations.

What ages of puppies are allowed into early puppy class? Puppy behavior starts to mature rapidly around five to six months of age for most breeds. Generally speaking, early puppy classes should be limited to dogs under six months old. Puppies between six and twelve months of age should have a separate class, where there is less off-leash play between puppies and more attention given to teaching puppies to focus more on their owners than on other dogs. These older puppies have already learned the lessons play teaches if they were socialized at an early age. If not, the optimal training window for those lessons has already closed and its better not to have your younger sporting dog puppy, who is just starting to learn those lessons, mixed in with such dogs. Although most sporting dog puppies continue to exhibit a strong desire to play with other dogs as they mature, it is critical they learn to exhibit self-control, not be allowed to pull over to other dogs, or to act silly in an inappropriate attempt to demand play. Only calm, polite behavior will earn the right to play with another dog and only then, if the other dog actually wants to play. Remember—it doesn't matter if your dog is friendly and wants to play with every other dog he meets. It is the dog who is being approached who should determine whether any social interaction occurs. Never allow your dog to force himself on other dogs. And if your puppy is afraid of an approaching dog, it's okay to prevent the other dog from approaching him.

Can I observe a class without my puppy? Any reputable trainer should allow you to observe a class without your puppy, provided you simply watch and don't attempt to participate or ask questions about your pup during class. Watch the dynamics between puppies, between puppies and owners, and between puppies, owners, and the instructor. Check out the physical layout of the class, how skirmishes are handled, and the teaching methods used in class. Does the instructor keep all the puppies safe during play? Is there a general atmosphere of respect in the class? How does your gut feel about the class? If you are uneasy about bringing your puppy to class, listen to your gut, even if you can't readily identify why you aren't comfortable with a particular training class. If you are uneasy, your puppy will sense that and become uneasy as well.

You might feel uncomfortable calling a trainer and asking these questions, but the impact early puppy classes can have over your sporting dog's lifetime is tremendous. It is crucial you pick the best class you can for him. A reputable trainer will welcome questions about his class and will appreciate the effort you put into finding the best training situation possible for your puppy.

What if I don't have a choice in classes?

If you don't have multiple options when it comes to early puppy classes for your sporting dog, interview the instructor of the only class anyway. Then decide, based on the answers you receive, if that class will be a good fit for you and your pup. If there are concerns, find out if the class can be adapted to fit your puppy's needs. Ultimately only you can decide if the risk of your puppy learning bad habits in an early puppy class outweighs the benefits of participating in that class. It takes more work on your part, but you can take your puppy around town to expose him to new environmental stimuli and, if you have access to friends with puppies or, more importantly, well-socialized adult dogs, you can make your own puppy play dates for socialization experiences. Your puppy can learn everything he needs to learn about proper canine communication from adult dogs who have good social skills. The adult dog should tolerate some play from the puppy (although he probably won't want to play as much as another puppy would) and, if the puppy needs to be corrected, he should give a correction and then stop as soon as the puppy alters his behavior appropriately. If you don't have access to socially-appropriate adult dogs or aren't sure if the dogs you are considering are actually appropriate, consult with the instructor. He should be able to help you find a good socialization partner for your pup. Remember to try to give your puppy as broad a range of dog experiences as possible so he learns to read dogs of different sizes, shapes, and personalities. There are many excellent books and training videos available to help you start to teach your young puppy basic manners. If you don't feel comfortable with the only early puppy class available to you, or you live in an area where there aren't any early puppy classes available at all, work on your own as best you can to socialize your sporting dog puppy and then enroll him in an older puppy class where playtime isn't included to help him learn manners.

Older puppy and adult class selection

Most larger puppies start showing adult behaviors around six months, when hormones begin kicking in and they enter their "teenager" phase. Play behaviors change significantly or begin to disappear altogether in most dog breeds, sexual behavior begins to increase, and arousal may start to tip over to serious altercations between puppies if not defused quickly and appropriately. Puppies that once played together wonderfully when they were three months old may start to have less tolerance for one another's antics as they mature. The need for continuous play with other dogs is no longer there; the critical brain development window for socialization has already closed. At this age, "playing" becomes more about learning self-control and tolerance around other dogs than chewing on and chasing every other dog around. Your teenaged pup should start to focus more on you than other puppies and dogs. Dogs mature mentally and physically at different rates, so individual developmental differences become more apparent between older puppies.

If older dogs are allowed to meet and play with each other, ask the instructor what purpose that interaction serves for your older sporting dog puppy or adult sporting dog. Teaching your dog to maintain self-control when in close proximity to other dogs and to pay attention to you instead of the dog are appropriate reasons to allow brief, controlled, on-leash interactions between adult dogs in class. But if your potential instructor tells you these encounters are supposed to teach your dog to play appropriately with other dogs, run, don't walk, away from that class. That is a potentially dangerous situation for your dog to be in. The window to learn how to play appropriately with other dogs closes at about sixteen weeks of age. Dogs really only learn, at best, how to tolerate other dogs after that point in their lives. Even if your adult dog is socially appropriate, if your instructor wants to teach adult dogs to play with each other, it is a safe bet that at least one of your dog's classmates has a social deficit. And if you own an adult social nerd and your instructor will tolerate his goofy sporting dog antics as an appropriate expression of "friendliness," your dog will continue to be reinforced for a behavior that may someday cause a fight to break out. Playtime between adult dogs should be done in a casual setting, between dogs that are known to get along. Adult playtime in class is risky and can cause irreparable harm.

What if my sporting dog was already an adult when I got him?

If you choose to adopt an adult sporting dog, it is important to understand that you may never be able to completely make up for any socialization deficits your dog already has, but you can certainly teach him coping skills to help him with these weak areas. As we discussed above, the prime window for learning social skills closes around four months of age. While an adult dog who wasn't properly socialized as a puppy can learn to tolerate the presence of other dogs and exhibit self-control, he may never be able to interact one-on-one with other dogs appropriately because of his lack of experience as a puppy. Or he may have had negative experiences with other dogs during the key learning period and so reacts negatively to other dogs. Don't worry about trying to figure out what might have happened to him before he came into your home. Instead, focus on learning about his behavior now and what you might be able to do to help him with any inappropriate behaviors he has as an adult. Begin to socialize him to his environment as if he was a puppy, providing him easy, safe, and pleasant experiences. And most importantly, be willing to accept that an adult sporting dog who didn't learn appropriate canine communication skills as a puppy may never be able to play appropriately with other dogs. And that's OK! Teach him to tolerate other dogs, but never try to force him to "play" with another dog. Chances are your dog won't end up learning anything positive from the experience and he may even end up getting hurt in the process. Your adult dog may be perfectly content to just hang out with you. And for most rescue dogs, that alone is a vast improvement in their lives!

A few words about dog parks and doggie daycare

Dog parks and doggie daycare facilities have become increasingly popular with urban dog owners. If dogs can be dropped off at daycare or turned loose in the dog park to "play" and "socialize," owners don't have to carve out time or make the physical effort to exercise their dogs themselves. On the surface, dog parks and daycare seem like the perfect solution to exercising and socializing dogs, and indeed they are, for some dogs. Most dogs come home happy and exhausted after spending time in either place. But before deciding to use a dog park or dog daycare to exercise your sporting dog, it is important to understand the risks associated with taking your dog to either place and to know how to decide if your dog is truly playing or if there are more dangerous pack interactions going on. Remember, proper social skills can only be learned from interacting with other dogs who already possess proper social skills. Is your sporting dog really learning how to behave appropriately around people and dogs when he is at the dog park or daycare running around with other dogs with unknown social skills?

Some dog owners, in particular those who think of their dogs as human child substitutes, often have a hard time accepting that most adult dogs don't need or want to "play" with other dogs in the same way they wanted to play as puppies. This is particularly true of many sporting dog owners, since most of these breeds retain an almost juvenile desire to play well into adulthood. Puppies play to practice the skills they would need to survive if they were in the wild. They stalk, chase, grab, and nip at each other to perfect the crucial pieces of the predatory behavior chain we looked at earlier. They also learn to "speak dog" to one another and interact appropriately with other dogs. Puppies undoubtedly enjoy playing with each other, but the primary purpose behind play is to learn survival and social skills. As puppies mature, the need for this type of interaction with other dogs naturally diminishes. Dogs who have been bred to work alone (like most terrier breeds) often lose the desire to play with other dogs far sooner than those dogs who have been bred to work more closely with other dogs and people (like retrievers) do. When socially-appropriate adult dogs who know each other get together, they are more likely to engage in casual environmental exploration and just "hanging out" together than in wrestling, chasing, and chewing on each other like puppies do. This is perfectly normal; no amount of exposure to other dogs is going to change that.

Barnum and Shocker used to wrestle and run together as puppies, but as adults, they enjoy spending time together in more sedate activities.

Because dogs are pack animals, any time two or more dogs are put together, a pack dynamic is created. This dynamic can become very dangerous very quickly. When you take your sporting dog to the dog park or put him in daycare, you have little or no control over the other dogs he will interact with. Play should always involve give and take between *all* the participants; a dog being chased should also have the chance to chase others. But many times, when unacquainted adult dogs are put together to "play," one or two dogs end up being singled out and chased mercilessly by the rest of the impromptu pack that forms. This is more of a hunting activity than a play activity for all involved. All the dogs certainly go home tired, but for different reasons. The dogs who were being chased are just as exhausted from the mental stress of not being able to escape as from the physical exercise; the dogs who were chasing are exhausted from the physical exercise and the arousal that chasing causes. But none of the dogs were actually "playing" and they have all learned undesirable social lessons. There is a very fine line between this type of "play" and actual predation. The dogs who couldn't escape are learning to fear other dogs and the dogs who chased are learning to be canine bullies. Putting a sporting dog in this type of "play" situation can be dangerous. Additionally, if your sporting dog is one of those dogs who acts silly around other dogs, he will be able to practice this inappropriate and potentially dangerous behavior with no intervention from you, making it even more difficult to ever change that behavior.

While it is true that many people take their sporting dogs to dog parks and daycares every day without any problems at all, the chances are still extremely high that someday the circumstances will be just right and your dog will have a negative experience. Are you willing to take that chance with your dog? Be sure you don't impose your desire for your dog to have canine friends unrealistically on your dog. Weigh the actual quality of life your dog would have without daycare and dog parks (from *his* point of view, not yours) against the risk that he will learn bad habits or get hurt before you decide to put him in either situation. Many behavioral problems that owners try to solve through daycare and dog parks can be more effectively altered simply by providing your dog more structured exercise at home and spending time actually training him. If you spend fifteen minutes driving to the dog park, fifteen minutes allowing your dog to run there, and another fifteen minutes driving back home, you have access to 45 minutes in your day, already devoted to your dog, to give him meaningful exercise with you and plenty of actual training to keep his mind healthy and teach him exactly what you would like him to do. That may be a better way to spend your time with your dog, particularly from your dog's point of view.

Chapter 5

How Do Dogs Learn?

The dog calls forth, on the one hand, the best that a human person is capable of—self-sacrificing devotion to a weaker and dependent being and, on the other hand, the temptation to exercise power in a willful and arbitrary, even perverse, manner. Both traits can exist in the same person.

~ Yi-Fu Tuan
Dominance & Affection: The Making of Pets

It can be challenging to live with a sporting dog. Instinctive sporting dog behaviors are often in direct contradiction with the behaviors we want in our pets and we may find ourselves spending tremendous amounts of time trying to teach our sporting dogs to stop acting like the dogs they are. The goal of dog training should never be to make our sporting dogs behave like furry, four-legged humans, but rather to help them behave appropriately as canine members of our family, while still allowing them to be the wonderful, unique dogs they are. Dogs don't think exactly the same way we do; they don't have the same problem-solving abilities, the same sense of "right" and "wrong," or even the same perception of time that we do. To effectively and humanely train a dog, we need to understand how dogs learn and then tailor our training methods to meet a sporting dog's unique needs so training will be pleasant for the living beings on both ends of the leash.

Learning theory overview

Learning theory is a vast, fascinating scientific field. There are many excellent books that delve into the myriad of details about how animals learn, such as Pamela Reid's *Excel-erated Learning*. In this chapter, we will look at just a few learning theory concepts that most directly impact the basic training we do with our sporting dogs. If you understand these concepts, you will learn how to communicate with your dog in a way that makes sense to him, so he will be able to learn what you want him to learn more quickly and easily.

Classical conditioning

Classical conditioning is one way dogs learn. This type of learning is what Pavlov saw in his research dogs and is how dogs learn the sound of a clicker means a reward is coming. Whenever Pavlov's dogs saw and smelled their food coming, they began to drool in anticipation of eating; drooling wasn't a response the dogs were taught to perform, but rather a natural physiological response by their bodies to get them ready to consume food. Pavlov noticed that after some time, the dogs began to drool at the sight of the kennel help, regardless of whether they were bringing food to the dogs or not. The dogs had associated the kennel help with the delivery of food, and started reacting to the kennel help in the same way they reacted to the sight of their meals. The kennel help had become what is known as a conditioned reinforcer. The arrival of the kennel help became associated with the arrival of food in the dogs' minds, whether or not food was actually present.

Operant conditioning

Operant conditioning is another mode of learning that is used in dog training. This type of learning happens when a dog makes an association between his behavior and the consequence that immediately follows that behavior. If the consequence that immediately follows the behavior is something the dog likes, the behavior is more likely to happen again. If the consequence that immediately follows the behavior is something the dog doesn't like, the behavior is not as likely to happen again. By controlling the consequences that follow a dog's behavior, you can affect the likelihood the behavior will happen in the future. If you've heard the term "positive reinforcement training," you've heard of operant conditioning.

Operant conditioning is typically divided into four quadrants, or variations, based on the way consequences are manipulated immediately following the behavior. The four quadrants are positive reinforcement, negative reinforcement, positive punishment and negative punishment. The terms "positive" and "negative" refer to *adding* (positive) or *subtracting* (negative) something from your dog's environment to influence the likelihood your dog will perform a particular behavior again. "Reinforcement" is anything that increases the likelihood a behavior will occur again, while "punishment" is anything that decreases the likelihood a behavior will occur again. Training sometimes involves crossing quadrants, so it is useful to have a basic understanding of what all four quadrants are and how they work. A reinforcer is anything your dog wants or needs from his environment; a punisher is anything your dog will seek to avoid in his environment.

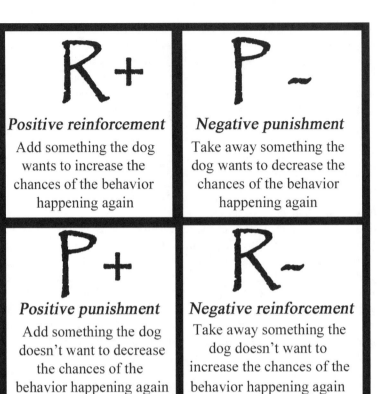

Understanding how operant conditioning works will help your training become more effective.

Positive reinforcement involves adding something to your dog's environment that your dog wants, immediately after the dog performs a desired behavior. By reinforcing your dog for a desired behavior, you increase the likelihood that the behavior will occur in the future. For example, if you say "Sit" and your dog sits, you might give him a treat he likes as a reinforcer for that behavior. The dog performed a desired behavior and you "added" a treat as a consequence of that behavior—you have used positive reinforcement to increase the likelihood that the next time you say "Sit," your dog will, in fact, sit. Most people are familiar with this type of operant conditioning (you probably already use this with your children or dogs), even if you were unaware of the scientific terminology involved.

Positive punishment involves adding something the dog wants to avoid to his environment when the dog performs an undesired behavior. This technique decreases the likelihood the behavior will occur in the future. The dog will change his behavior to avoid the unpleasant addition to his environment. This is the way many people used to train their dogs. For example, if you say "Sit" and your dog stands there and stares at you instead of sitting, you give him a sharp slap on the rump to get him to sit. By adding a punisher to your dog's environment when he performs an incorrect behavior (slap on the rump for standing instead of sitting), you decrease the chances that your dog will stand instead of sit the next time you say "Sit." Your dog performs the correct behavior to avoid something he finds unpleasant when you train using positive punishment. Unfortunately, while he may sit the next time to avoid the slap, he might also shake with fear as he does it.

Negative punishment involves subtracting something the dog wants when the dog performs an undesired behavior. This technique also decreases the likelihood the behavior will occur again in the future. Let's say you have a rule that your dog must sit before anyone can pet him. As a person approaches your dog to pet him, you tell your dog "Sit." Instead of promptly sitting, he just stands there, staring at the approaching person, making no move to sit. Your dog clearly wants to be petted by that person and has tuned you completely out. Since your dog didn't perform the desired behavior (sit), you ask the person to immediately turn and walk away instead of petting your dog. Now you are using negative punishment to decrease the likelihood that the next time you say "Sit," your dog will stand instead. You took what the dog wants (the approaching person) away because the dog performed an undesired behavior (stand). Most of us tend to think of punishment as a physical correction of some type, but losing the chance to be petted can be an effective punishment for a dog that really enjoys interacting with people.

Negative reinforcement involves subtracting something the dog wants to avoid from his environment when the dog performs a correct behavior. This technique increases the likelihood the behavior will occur in the future. Using this quadrant of operant conditioning, when you say "Sit," you also immediately give a sharp collar correction upward, putting unpleasant pressure on your dog's neck. As soon as your dog's rear hits the floor, you release the pressure. You removed something the dog wanted to avoid (pressure on his neck) when the dog performed the desired behavior (sit), thereby increasing the likelihood that your dog will sit the next time you say "Sit."

Which quadrants work best with a sporting dog?

If you understand the basics of operant conditioning, you understand why various training techniques work and how to fairly and effectively go about training your dog. Although all four quadrants of learning theory will work to increase desired behaviors and diminish undesired behaviors, most of the time using positive reinforcement is what works best. Historically, many sporting dog trainers who worked with dogs actually used for hunting relied heavily on positive punishment to "break" dogs to hunt. Harsh physical methods were used to teach dogs to retrieve with a soft mouth (i.e., to hold a bird but not crunch it or eat it), to stay in gun range, and to come when called in from the field. Fortunately, many trainers now understand operant conditioning better and rely on much more positive methods to train working sporting dogs. By giving a dog something he wants in exchange for performing a behavior that you want, you establish a respectful working relationship that you can readily manipulate to bring out the best in your dog. In addition to being more learner-friendly and humane quadrants to work in, working with positive reinforcement and negative punishment is less likely to trigger adverse behavioral responses than working with negative reinforcement and positive punishment is.

Since this isn't a book on learning theory, we will use the term "reward" instead of "reinforcer," and "correction" instead of "punisher," for the remainder of the book. Although not technically correct, most people use "reward" and "correction" interchangeably with "reinforcer" and "punisher" in everyday dog training discussions, so those are the terms we will use as well.

The four stages of learning

Regardless of which quadrant of operant conditioning is used to teach a behavior, learning a new behavior is rarely an instantaneous event. Most learning occurs in stages, over time. It is important to keep these stages in mind so you can maintain the behaviors you taught your dog in training class long after the class has ended.

The first step in learning any new behavior involves acquiring new knowledge. This is the step most of us think of when we think about "learning." The second step involves using that new knowledge until the learner is fluent, or automatic, in its use. The third step involves applying this new knowledge to other situations where it is relevant. The fourth step involves maintaining the knowledge for the learner's lifetime so that the knowledge becomes part of the behavioral repertoire of the learner.

Let's look again at the steps involved in teaching your dog to sit. When you first introduce this concept to your dog, he has no idea what the word "Sit" means. He must learn how to lift his head up and back, shift his weight back, lower his rump all the way to the floor, tuck his feet underneath himself, and move his tail into a comfortable position, all just to perform the simple behavior we call "Sit." Initially you will have to help him figure out how to accomplish all this. It takes a lot of mental concentration for your dog to focus on what you want and move all his body parts correctly. He is acquiring new knowledge and is in the first step of the learning process.

Robin uses a treat and physical help to show Calley how to sit by luring her into position during the first stage of learning this behavior.

Eventually, with enough repetitions and experience, your sporting dog starts sitting on his own when you say the word "Sit." His actions become automatic when you say that word and he can begin to perform this behavior reliably. You don't have to help him into a sit now; he knows how to move his body into position. He is at the second step of learning and is becoming fluent in performing a sit behavior.

As Calley gains fluency with the sit behavior, Robin no longer needs to use a lure or physical help to get her into position.

As your dog obtains even more experience with "Sit," you start asking him to perform that behavior in different places or around different distractions. You ask for the behavior outside in the yard, in the park, or while someone comes through your front door. You are broadening your dog's experience with "Sit" and asking him to perform that behavior in many different situations. This is the third step in the learning process, where your dog learns that "Sit" means "Sit," no matter where he is or what is going on. Bob Bailey, a world-renowned animal trainer with decades of experience training many different species, points out that when you teach an animal a new behavior, you spend approximately 10% of your time actually teaching the behavior, and 90% of your time developing the animal's environmental confidence so he learns to perform the behavior any time, any place. In competitive obedience training, this is referred to as "proofing" the behavior.

This stage of learning is often the one that dog owners skip over, when it really should be the one that is given the most time and effort. Dogs don't generalize new learned behaviors to different situations very well; they have to be shown that "Sit" means "Sit" whether you are in the living room, the front yard, or at the park. Learning to sit in one environment doesn't automatically mean your dog will understand how to sit in a different one. This is why so many dogs will do beautiful sits at home, but can't do a single sit when they come to class. The dogs haven't generalized the sit behavior outside their homes yet. We will be using the 80% rule to help determine when a dog is ready to face more difficult training challenges as his fluency increases.

Integrating the sit behavior into your dog's everyday life is the fourth stage of learning. If you ask your dog to sit as a regular part of his lifestyle, your dog will continue to perform that behavior for the rest of his life. If, however, you quit asking for the behavior as soon as your training class ends, it will soon weaken and your dog will eventually begin to perform it less reliably. It isn't enough to spend a few weeks out of your dog's life teaching him to sit, down, and walk politely on-leash; you have to incorporate these behaviors into your sporting dog's everyday life to keep them strong. The more difficult the behavior is for your dog to perform, the quicker it will deteriorate if you quit asking him to perform it on a regular basis.

The 80% rule

Sometimes it is difficult to decide when to make the training more difficult for your sporting dog as his fluency increases. One handy yardstick to use when deciding when to add more difficult challenges to the training environment is the 80% rule. Ask your dog to perform whatever behavior you are working on five times in a training session. *If* your dog can perform the behavior: 1) the *first* time; 2) with a *single* cue; 3) in the *way you want* the behavior performed; 4) four out of five times (80%), he is probably ready for you to make the training a little more difficult so that his behavioral fluency will continue to improve. Be honest! There is no prize for trying to force your dog to handle distractions that he isn't ready for yet. If you cheat in your behavioral analysis of your dog, you will slow down your training. It's OK if he can't do the behavior four out of five times when you test him. Just keep working at that same level of difficulty until he can be successful at least 80% of the time. If he can't perform the behavior at all with the distractions that are around, then you've already made the environment too difficult for him; make the environment less distracting and work awhile longer on the behavior until he is truly ready to move on to more difficult distractions.

> # If 4 out of 5 times Your dog responds just fine, You can change something in your training, But only one thing at a time!

Keeping the 80% rule in mind will help you keep your dog's training moving forward efficiently.

Knowing vs. doing

Training a dog always involves a certain amount of guesswork, especially when you expect a dog to behave one way and he behaves another way instead. You must rely on the imperfect method of observing his outward behavior to guess whether or not learning has actually occurred, since you have no way to peek inside his skull and see the microscopic changes that occur in the brain as learning physically takes place. But if the dog performs the correct behavior on a single cue at least 80% of the time we ask him to perform it, you can reasonably infer he has, in fact, learned that behavior (at least in the particular environment he was tested in). Even so, you are dealing with a living, thinking, feeling, independent animal and there is no guarantee he will perform that behavior each and every time he is cued to do so, no matter how well trained he is. No human is 100% perfect performing any learned behavior, so why would you expect your dog to be 100% perfect?

Many things affect whether a dog will perform a learned behavior. The dog might not be feeling well, something in the environment might be interfering with his ability to perform the behavior, or he might not understand that he can perform the behavior in that particular environment. A dog also might not perform a learned behavior simply because he isn't motivated enough to perform at that particular moment. Motivation reflects what is most important to a dog at any given point in time and the amount of effort he is willing to put into gaining what is important to him. Lack of motivation doesn't mean a dog chooses to avoid performing a behavior just to "get even" with you for something that happened earlier in the day or because he wants to "make you mad." It simply means that from your dog's point of view, there isn't enough value in gaining the reward or avoiding the correction for him to perform the learned behavior you asked him to perform. He may "know" how to perform the behavior, but still not "do" it because the motivation isn't there. Learning how to effectively motivate your dog will help you train your dog more easily; we will look at that concept very closely in the next chapter.

Management vs. training

In addition to actually teaching our dogs how to behave, we must also use environmental and behavioral management techniques to facilitate the initial learning process, especially when trying to replace undesired behaviors with more appropriate ones. Simply put, management in dog training involves manipulating a dog's environment to influence his behavior. It can provide a "quick fix" for many problem behaviors so you can retain your sanity while working through the slower process of training new desired behaviors. Your dog doesn't learn how to behave appropriately by management alone, but you can often get immediate behavioral results that will help the learning process if you incorporate management techniques along with training.

Let's say you have a sporting dog who, for several years, has been allowed to jump on anyone who walks through your door. Now you are trying to teach him to sit politely when guests come into your home. You must train your dog to sit, to stay in that position until released, and to ignore people coming into your home. That's a lot to learn! To speed up the learning process and minimize confusion, you should train the new door greeting behaviors, while simultaneously preventing him from continuing to jump on guests through management. There are many different ways to manage your dog's behavior so he can't jump on people. Putting him on a leash so you can physically control him *before* your guests come in or putting him in another room when guests arrive so he doesn't even have access to them until he has calmed down are just two options to manage his door greeting behavior. You are removing the opportunity for him to continue to do what you no longer want him to do through management. If you allow him to continuing jumping on people at the door while simultaneously trying to train him to sit when guests arrive, you will confuse him. If you don't have time to train, you must at least manage the environment so the old behaviors can't be practiced, if you want your dog to eventually learn a new behavior that is reliable. Training takes time, particularly when you are trying to change a behavior your dog has engaged in for a long time. If you prevent your dog from doing the undesired behavior while you are also teaching him a desired behavior, you will change his behavior more quickly and minimize frustration for both of you.

Environmental management is also an easy way to keep dogs from learning bad habits in the first place. If shoes are put away where your dog can't get to them, he can never learn that chewing on them is fun. If he is never allowed to jump on company, he's not as likely to do that to get attention. Having your dog drag a long line when running in the yard will keep him from playing keep away from you when you want him to come in. Managing your dog's environment so that he is only able to do what you want him to do is a relatively easy way to develop good behaviors in your dog. But, of course, reality sometimes prevents us from managing our dog's environment that closely. Children (and spouses!) may forget to put shoes in the closet, guests may encourage your dog to jump up on them or your dog may sneak out of the door without a long line on. In spite of your best intentions, your dog may develop bad habits. But if you develop a good training plan and combine that with the most consistent environmental management possible in your home, you can nip bad habits in the bud and help your sporting dog behave in ways that make him a true joy to have as part of the family.

Chapter 6

Becoming More Interesting Than Birds in the Eyes of Your Sporting Dog

---

The dog's agenda is simple, fathomable, overt: I want. "I want to go out, come in, eat something, lie here, play with that, kiss you." There are no ulterior motives with a dog, no mind games, no second-guessing, no complicated negotiations or bargains, and no guilt trips or grudges if a request is denied.

~ Caroline Knapp
American author

Now that we've explored how dogs learn and how to use rewards and corrections effectively in training, let's figure out exactly what motivates *your* sporting dog so you can start building up a collection of effective tools to use for training.

Sporting dog cost/benefit analysis

Dogs are quite adept at cost/benefit analysis. Imagine that you have spent months carefully training your sporting dog to come to you on a single cue when he hears the word "Come." You've built his fluency through hundreds of repetitions and have practiced in many different places to help him generalize the behavior. His reward has always been to come inside with you when he gets to you and, once inside, he gets praise and a scratch behind the ears. However, for some reason, you haven't ever practiced this recall behavior when birds were around. So one day your dog is standing out in the middle of your back yard, staring at a bird in a tree. You step outside and call "Come!" expecting him to stop staring and come running to you. But instead of coming to you, he continues to stare at the bird; in fact, he doesn't even look at you. He just keeps staring at the bird.

You might think your dog is just "blowing you off," being "bad," or "getting even" with you for not letting him play outside earlier in the day. But that isn't the case; he is simply telling you exactly what is most valuable to him at that moment in time—watching the bird. It is more satisfying and valuable to him to continue his instinct-driven hunting behavior than it is to come to you and go inside the house. Nothing you have offered your dog to date, including coming into the house, is more valuable to *him* than hunting for birds. From *his* perspective, why on Earth would he want to leave his bird to come to you, just so you can take him inside and end all his hunting fun? The cost/benefit analysis for this situation tips the odds against you getting him to leave the bird and come to you. Without proper motivation, your dog will never have a truly reliable recall around birds (or anything else that *really* interests him).

Learn to look at your sporting dog's behavior (desired *and* undesired) as a source of information about what motivates your dog, rather than an emotional battle of wills. Dogs don't lie about what they find interesting or rewarding. Simply put, you must be more rewarding to your dog than all the other things competing for his attention at any given moment in time, if you want your dog to reliably perform whatever behavior you ask him to do. Of course, it isn't possible to be more rewarding than the rest of the world 100% of the time, but you can certainly find ways to become more valuable to your dog in situations that are important to you. By taking the information your dog gave you about the relative value of hunting birds as compared to coming to you to go inside, you may be able to make changes in your training rewards so that you can become more valuable to him than a bird. This change isn't about treats or leashes, but rather about being the gatekeeper for access to all good things for your dog, including birds. Through you, your dog can earn access to the things he want in his life. Building up a collection of verbal, physical, and environmental rewards that are very motivating to your sporting dog will help you become that gatekeeper. The rest of this chapter will help you build your collection by examining the who, what, where, when, why, and how of rewards.

Who determines what can be used as a reward?

In order to become more interesting than birds in your sporting dog's eyes, you have to identify rewards that will motivate your dog to work with you. Who determines what these rewards are? Your dog, of course! It doesn't matter how interesting you think a toy is or how well a certain type of treat has worked as a reward for someone else's dog. If *your* dog isn't motivated enough to work for that particular treat or toy, you can't use it as a reward. Similarly, your dog also determines what constitutes a correction. If you frown at your dog and he rolls on his back and submissively urinates, you know that your body language is a powerful correction from his point of view, even if you didn't *intend* to correct him with your unhappy appearance. Training your sporting dog will go much more quickly and successfully if you remember your dog is the one in charge of identifying potential rewards and corrections.

What can be used as a reward?

Practically everything your dog wants in his life! Most dog owners think of praise or treats when they think of rewards, but this is only the very tip of the reward iceberg. Think like your sporting dog and all of a sudden the world becomes one gigantic cookie jar filled with countless rewards (most of them free) for you to use! Watch what your dog chooses to pay attention to when he is left alone to do whatever he wants. Dogs don't lie about what interests them, so why waste time guessing at what your dog might be willing to work for, when he is showing you these things all the time? As long as it is safe for both you and your dog, access to it can be controlled, it can promptly be delivered and is practical to use, almost anything that interests your dog can be used as a reward. With careful observation, you can begin to build a collection of non-food rewards to use when training. You can even include "naughty" things in your reward list, too—hunting birds, digging a hole, and jumping up can all be used as rewards, as long as *you* start and end the "naughty" behavior on *your* terms and only after your dog has performed a behavior for you.

Food

Most of us are familiar with using dog treats to train dogs. Food is a powerful intrinsic motivator; we don't typically have to encourage a healthy dog to eat. Every healthy dog alive today is food motivated to some extent, since he is obviously motivated to eat enough food to survive. With a little creativity and perseverance, you can find some type of food to use during training with even the most finicky eater. Treats are often the first type of reward we use when teaching our dogs a new behavior because they can be given quickly and are relatively easy to use during training sessions.

Be creative when considering treats to use for training. For sporting dogs who aren't picky about what they eat, you have a whole range of treat options available. Experiment with a selection of treats to see which ones really interest your dog. Instead of pre-packaged dog treats, try treats like skinless chicken, string cheese, homemade dog treats, dried apples, sweet potato chips, raw carrot slices, dehydrated beef heart, blueberry bagels, green tripe, dried squid, or anything else you can think of that is safe for your dog to eat. Never give your dog food containing chocolate, cocoa, raisins, onions, xylitol (an artificial sweetener commonly found in chewing gum), or high amounts of fat or salt. For dogs with severe food allergies, you can try to get his regular diet in an alternative form for use when training. For example, if you feed a special kibble diet, see if that same diet is available in a canned version which you can let the dog lick off a spoon as a training reward; alternatively, there are dog treat recipes available on-line that use ground kibble instead of flour that can be adapted to make special dietary needs training treats. If you truly have a finicky eater who is not even interested in cooked chicken or beef with excess fat removed, low fat cheese cubes, or water-packed tuna, you can use the dog's regular kibble as a reward. Since your dog eats enough to stay alive, his regular food should work as a last ditch food reward. Remember, no matter how tasty *you* might think a particular treat is or should be, it is your *dog* who is in charge of deciding which treats will work best as food rewards, and which treats will work in stressful situations.

In addition to taking your dog's food preferences into account when selecting treats, it is also important to keep in mind how easy the treats will be to prepare, carry around for training, break into appropriately-sized tiny training tidbits without leaving behind messy crumbs, actually give to the dog, and how many you can give during a training session without upsetting your dog's stomach or making him thirsty. Create a mix of several different treats your dog likes and you will have considerable flexibility when training. Because stress tends to reduce a dog's desire to eat, the treats that work well at home for training may not do the trick under the stress of training classes; having some real meat or cheese options in your goodie bag will usually overcome the normal amounts of stress your dog may feel in class and allow you to use treats effectively there. Regardless of the types of treats you use, spend a few moments before training to break up your treats into tiny pieces, toss them in a plastic baggie to keep your training bag or pocket clean and you will be ready to train!

Less is more when using food as a training reward. A treat should simply be a taste of something special, not an entire meal in every bite! Similar to the human fast food industry, the portion size of most pre-packaged dog treats is far larger than appropriate for use as a training treat. Even for larger sporting dogs, a treat reward should only be about the size of the tip of your little finger or a green pea. Your dog should be able to eat it in a second or two, with little, if any, chewing required. By keeping the treat size small, you will be able to train longer before your dog gets bored with the treat or actually gets physically full. You can also use richer, more calorie-dense treats without making your dog fat or upsetting his stomach, because you are only giving very tiny portions of these treats during a training session. If you use raw foods as treats, be sure to handle them carefully to avoid spreading food-borne illnesses. Freeze tiny training session portions so you thaw and use up the entire portion in one session to minimize problems. If you are using cheese sticks, cut the sticks into several sections and only take one section out of the refrigerator at a time. And, regardless of the treats you are using, be sure to remove any leftovers from your pockets after your training session is finished to protect your clothes from dog teeth and your washing machine from a gooey mess!

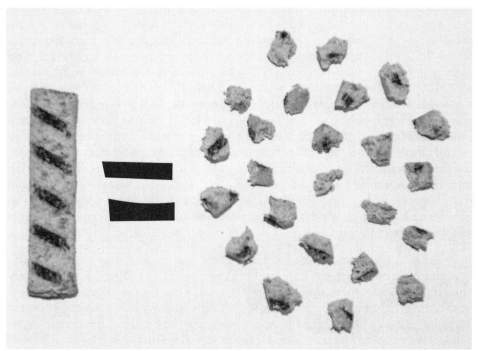

This one pre-packaged treat can easily be broken into two dozen training-sized treats.

Toys

Toys are also potentially powerful rewards for sporting dogs if they are used correctly. Think outside the traditional toy box when identifying sporting dog toys; toys can be anything you and your dog can safely interact with together. Just because you wouldn't think of an item as a toy doesn't mean your dog won't see it as the greatest thing in the world to play with! Pay attention to the objects your dog chooses to play with on his own. Not all of them will be well-suited to use for training, but you might find a few options. Your dog is in charge of toy selection—your job is to be sure the toy can be used safely and that the toy is only used under your supervision.

Texture, sound, motion, and "carryability" are four characteristics that influence toy desirability for sporting dogs. Most sporting dogs are interested in anything that mimics prey behavior or that can easily and comfortably be carried around. Soft, squeaky, furry toys that can be moved around in an erratic manner like a prey animal and can withstand the wear and tear of being carried around and repeatedly retrieved are good toy choices for most sporting dogs. Hard toys like Kongs® and certain other hard plastic toys aren't appropriate for training rewards because you will be delivering the toy as quickly as possible following his correct behavior, which may mean you "toss" the toy toward your dog. If he catches a hard toy, his teeth might get damaged; if he doesn't catch it, he will get hit in the face and might get hurt or scared. Keep the hard toys out for chewing, and use soft plastic, fabric, fleece, or rubber toys for training.

When making your training toy selection, keep in mind how easy it will be to carry and conceal the toy from your dog during training, to hold on to the toy while your dog plays with it, and how messy it will be after your dog covers it in drool. And expect that your dog will destroy a few toys over his lifetime. Toys are meant to be enjoyed, so buy some inexpensive ones with little or no stuffing and don't worry if they get worn out or destroyed during training.

When you play with toys as training rewards, you must be able to control the play so your dog doesn't grab his toy and take off, prematurely ending his training session. No matter how valuable the toy might be for your dog and how hard he will work to get it, it is pointless to use it as a reward if your dog takes off the first time you give it to him and then plays keep away from you. That may be very fun for him, but it ruins your training session. If you are using a toy as a reward and your dog will try to take off with it, either the toy or your sporting dog must be on a leash at all times so you can keep control of the situation. For example, if your dog absolutely loves tennis balls but doesn't have a reliable retrieve, either train your sporting dog on a long line (20 feet long or more) so you can let him chase his ball and then use the long line to guide him back to you if he tries to run away, or, poke a hole through a tennis ball and thread a long piece of rope through it so you can get your dog to return it back to you by reeling in the ball with the rope. Either way, you will be able to use the ball as a reward and, with minimal disruption, do several training repetitions without having your dog run away with it.

Allowing sporting dogs to tug on their toys often receives a bad rap because owners worry their dogs will become aggressive or "hard-mouthed." People who hunt with their sporting dogs want them to be gentle when holding game and don't encourage the dogs to bite hard or hold on to anything forcefully. But for the average, non-hunting pet dog, tug is an acceptable game to play, as long as you can start and end the game safely and on your terms, not your dog's terms. Just keep in mind that you don't want your dog to become so excited he can no longer think or listen to you when playing tug. Control the tempo of the play through your own body language—if you want to slow things down, quit moving around with the toy. Become silent and still and use a very calm voice. If you want to rev your dog up a little more, become more animated yourself and talk in a more excited voice. Keep the tugging low and slow. Your dog's feet should stay on the ground and you should move the toy around slowly side-to-side when your dog is tugging on it; you risk seriously injuring your dog's neck and spine if you pick him up off his feet while he is hanging onto the toy or if you snap his head around quickly. And be sure you actually let your dog tug for a few moments if you are using the toy as a reward. If you shove the toy in your dog's face, then yank it away as soon as your dog grabs at it, he will soon lose interest in the game because he isn't getting the chance to play with the toy.

Karen engages Keagen appropriately in a game of tug as a training reward.

Many sporting dogs aren't naturally interested in tugging; the instinct to be gentle with objects in their mouths and a willingness to defer to their owners and give objects up sometimes overrides the desire to grab hard and hold on for dear life. There are so many other games you can play with your dog, its okay to not force your dog to play tug if he really doesn't want to tug.

No dog enjoys having a toy shoved in his face repeatedly, particularly if it isn't even a toy he likes. That's not playing with your dog—that's assaulting him! An easy way to invite your sporting dog to play with any toy is to ask yourself "What would a bird or bunny do?" and then move his toy around accordingly. Your dog is hard-wired to be aroused by these types of movements, so the more you can make a toy act like an animal, the more likely your sporting dog will be interested in it. A bunny in your yard typically runs a little on the ground, pauses, runs a little more, maybe makes a little noise or digs in the dirt for a bit, then dashes off in an erratic path for the nearest fence or hiding spot if your sporting dog suddenly starts chasing it. This type of play requires you to be actively involved in the play as well. Playing with your dog will help your relationship tremendously. You will have the opportunity to work on any bite inhibition issues that may exist, teach your dog self-control, and reinforce the idea that *you* provide all the fantastic stuff in your dog's life, like his toys. Besides that, it's just plain fun to have a good game with your dog and, as an added bonus, if you are holding on to one end of the toy while he plays with it, you don't have to worry about him running off with it before you teach him how to retrieve!

Verbal and physical interaction

Most of the rewards your sporting dog receives for performing the behaviors you ask of him should come directly from you. Because you will always have your hands and your voice with you when you are interacting with your dog, it is definitely worth the time and effort it takes to identify ways to talk to and touch your dog to motivate and reward him for correct behavior.

Verbal interaction with your dog can be a powerful reinforcer, if you take the time to build value into your voice. Humans are verbal creatures and we often verbally interact with our dogs as if they are also human. Because we use our voices so much, our dogs (just like children and spouses!) often learn to tune us out. They hear us all the time, so our voices aren't special. Verbal rewards are only effective if you change the pitch, tone, or presentation of your voice so it stands out against the routine verbal barrage we inflict on our dogs. Higher pitched, "squeaky" sounds delivered in a quiet manner often catch a sporting dog's ear, presumably because these sounds are similar to prey sounds. Verbally praising your dog in a higher-pitched voice than normal will help the praise stand out against the background noise. This doesn't mean you have to "baby talk" (although a lot of dogs *love* that type of talk), but just raise the pitch a little when you praise. Predators also tune in to the quiet sounds of prey moving in the environment; many times quiet praise gets more attention than loud praise. You have the ability to reward any behavior any time with praise since you always have your voice with you, so it is definitely worth learning how to talk to your dog in a way that is truly rewarding to him.

You can also influence your dog's emotional state by the way you talk to him. For example, if you say "Good dog!!" in a high-pitched, upbeat manner, your dog will probably act excited by the praise. But if you say "G-o-o-o-d dog" in a low-pitched, slow, drawn-out manner, your dog may very well start to relax. The speed and pitch of your praise needs to reflect the desired emotional response you want from your dog. Creating emotional associations with particular phrases and styles of praise can be very useful when you are training. Happy and excited praise can be used for active behaviors, such as coming when called, and soothing praise can be used for static behaviors, such as staying in one spot. The old adage "It's not *what* you say, but *how* you say it" is very true in dog training, so experiment with your voice to find a verbal style that gets your dog's attention and rewards him for correct behavior.

Developing truly pleasurable forms of physical contact and play with sporting dogs can be a little trickier than developing rewarding verbal skills. You need to balance motivating your dog against over-exciting him; these dogs are eager to work with people and can sometimes be easy to over-arouse. Although there are always individual exceptions, most sporting dogs enjoy prolonged physical contact. But there are many different ways to actually pet your dog. Watch him while you pet him. Does he really seem to enjoy the contact, or is he merely tolerating being petted? Lip licking, pinning his ears back, ducking slightly to avoid contact, and vigorous shaking after you get done petting him are all subtle signs of stress that suggest your dog might not really be enjoying the type of physical contact you are giving him. Experiment with various ways to pet your sporting dog and watch his behavior closely to find out exactly how *he* enjoys being touched. You may find he enjoys being scratched at the base of the tail or behind the ears, but doesn't really enjoy being patted on the head or stroked down his back. You may also find that certain types of physical contact get him too excited to maintain self-control. Physical contact with your dog is a handy reward because as long as you have a hand free, you have way to reward your dog without making him lose control.

You can also use your hands to play with your sporting dog, as long as you are careful to keep the play relatively slow and controlled so he can maintain self-control. Sporting dogs are built for physical work and many find physical play very satisfying. Try pushing your sporting dog gently away from you in a playful manner and see if he comes popping right back toward you, asking for more. If he does, you can use that type of play to reward him; if he doesn't, mark that off your list of potential rewards. If he tries to bite you, stop immediately; he is too aroused.

Environmental rewards

Most of us are familiar with using treats, toys, praise, and pats for rewards, but when we expand our definition of a reward to include anything our dogs are willing to work for, our reward list becomes nearly limitless! The easiest way to develop a list of possible environmental rewards to use when training is to simply pay attention to what your dog likes to do when he's just hanging out, "being a dog." Being allowed to go outside, sniffing pee-mail at the corner fire hydrant, hunting birds, sleeping on the couch, and a myriad of other interactions with the environment can all be used as rewards when you are training your sporting dog. For example, if you ask your dog to give you eye contact when you are out for a walk and he does, you can immediately release him with a cue word to go read his pee-mail on the fire hydrant for a few moments as his reward for giving you attention. Allowing your dog time to simply be a dog is very reinforcing and can be a powerful reward. It also provides a mental health boost for your dog. No matter how well trained he is, your dog is still a dog and needs a chance to just be a dog sometimes. As long as you can control your dog's access to what he wants so he only gets it after he's performed the correct behavior, and the item is safe for both you and your dog to interact with, you can theoretically use it as a reward.

You can also use other trained behaviors as rewards, too. If your sporting dog loves to retrieve, you can cue him to sit and, as soon as he does, release him to retrieve a ball. Soon he will be as excited to sit as he is to retrieve, because he will associate the sit with the reward of being allowed to retrieve. This type of reward is very useful if you are training your sporting dog for a competitive dog sport; you can string multiple behaviors together, using ones your sporting dog really enjoys as rewards for ones he doesn't enjoy as much.

To use environmental rewards successfully, name the various things you decide to use. This will help you make clear to your dog when he is allowed to have a particular environmental reward and when he isn't allowed to have it. For example, suppose your sporting dog loves to "read pee-mail" left by other dogs at the corner fire hydrant. You have identified the hydrant as a potential effective reward because you know he really likes to sniff it. You can use this as an environmental reward because you can keep him from pulling over to the hydrant on his own when you are walking past, it is safe for him to interact with, and you have a way to "give" the hydrant to him as a reward for correct behavior, simply by allowing him to go over to it. To make it clear to your dog when he can read pee-mail and when he can't, it is helpful to name the reward. When you are walking past the hydrant and you aren't using it as a reward, simply keep walking and don't allow your dog to go over to it. Hold the leash short and, if necessary, move further away from the hydrant as you pass it so your dog doesn't get to sniff it. But when you want to use the hydrant as a reward, ask your dog for a behavior and, immediately after he performs the correct behavior, tell him "Good dog! Now go read your pee-mail!" and release him to sniff the hydrant. He might be confused at first, especially if you haven't usually been allowing him to sniff the hydrant. Go over to the hydrant with him and encourage him to sniff it. If you are consistent in saying nothing about the hydrant when you don't want him to sniff it and telling him to read his pee mail when you want him to sniff, he will eventually understand the difference. You will be able to use the hydrant as a reward instead of worrying that your dog will pull your arm off trying to get to it every time you walk past. And as an added bonus, if you actually let him sniff the hydrant once in awhile, it won't be quite so interesting to him anymore. Forbidden objects are always more intriguing than ones that are more readily accessible. By using distractions as rewards, we can actually decrease the power some distractions hold over our dogs.

*Bode likes to play with running water, so Luke and Grace
reward her with a drink from the pump for a good recall.*

When should the reward be given?

Timing is critical to effective dog training, so you need to be on your toes when you
work with your dog. One of the easiest ways to improve your timing is simply to get
organized before you start your training session. Have your rewards readily accessible
before you start asking for behaviors. If you are using treats as rewards and can't get
your hand in your pocket easily, keep them in a treat bag or put them in a bowl on a
nearby table so you can grab them quickly. Have them cut into small pieces and ready
to go. If you are using a toy as a reward, have it in your pocket, your waist band, or
your arm pit, ready to be tossed out. If you are going to let your dog outside as his
reward, make sure you are training by the door so you can immediately let him out.
If you can't get to the rewards quickly or something happens spontaneously that you
want to reward, you can always immediately reward your dog with praise and physical
interaction for a job well done. Every other type of reward needs to be prepared before
training starts; the quicker you reward a correct behavior, the quicker your dog will
learn to associate his behavior with earning his reward.

Where should the reward be given?

Dogs associate rewards and corrections most strongly with what they are performing at
the very moment they receive the reward or correction, so it is important to pay attention to what your dog is actually doing when you give him his reward. For example, if

you are working on teaching your sporting dog to sit and using a treat as the reward for a correct performance, you should deliver the treat in a way that allows him to get it without standing up. If you hold the treat away from your dog and he has to get up and walk a few steps to get the treat, you are rewarding the walking behavior more strongly than the sitting behavior, because he is actively walking at the precise moment he gets his treat. If you put the treat right down in front of his mouth so he can eat it while he is still sitting, you are rewarding the sit position, because he is sitting at the moment he gets his treat. Pay attention to where you dog is when he gets his reward; the position should enhance what you are actually trying to teach your dog. This will boost the power of each reward tremendously and speed up the learning process considerably.

Karen wants Keagan to walk right beside her left leg, so she delivers his rewards right next to her leg as they walk to help him understand proper walking position.

How should rewards be delivered?

How you deliver rewards is also important. When you deliver any reward besides physical contact, be sure to touch your sporting dog before and during the delivery. This helps build up the idea in his mind that you are quite literally connected with every reward in the universe, no matter what form that reward comes in. So slightly before or simultaneous with giving a treat, make sure you give your dog a light pat or a quick scratch.

Match the duration of the reward to the effort your dog puts forth to perform the behavior. The longer your dog has to concentrate on performing a behavior, or the more difficult the behavior is for him to perform, the longer the reward delivery should last. Combining different types of rewards is an easy way to increase the length of time your dog is rewarded for his behavior; combine a small treat with lots of verbal praise and physical contact to prolong the reward. Make a treat reward last longer by breaking it into even smaller pieces and feeding them one at a time to him. Aim to mark very special efforts with a full thirty seconds of reward to maximize the impact on your dog's training. This type of special reward session is often called a jackpot; think of it as the canine equivalent of being given a bonus for working extra hard on a special project at work. Jackpots should be used sparingly, just for those special moments when your dog has had a training breakthrough or performs a behavior phenomenally well. Since most people aren't good at guessing how long thirty seconds really is, sing the Final Jeopardy song from the TV game show Jeopardy to yourself while you reward your dog (or sing it out loud if that makes you and your dog happier!).

Toys used for training rewards should never be freely accessible to your dog when he isn't actually working with you to earn them. If your dog can play with his favorite toys any time he chooses simply by going to the toy box and picking one out, the value of those toys as training rewards is greatly diminished. Why should he work to earn a toy that he can go get any time he wants it without doing anything? Any toy you've identified as a possible training reward should be put away so your dog no longer has free access to it. Your dog will still get to play with it, but only after he has done something for you to earn that toy. If you are working on teaching him to give you eye contact on cue, you can cue your dog to watch you, and if he gives you eye contact, you can give him his favorite toy as his reward. Since absence makes the heart grow fonder, your dog will be quite willing to work for his toy because he wants the toy, but no longer has free access to it. Likewise, if you give your sporting dog a tasty treat "just because," every time you pass by the treat jar regardless of what he is doing at the time you give him the treat, his motivation to do something you want him to do just to earn that same treat will rapidly fade. But if you give him a treat only after he has done something you asked him to do, he will be much more motivated to work for you to earn his treat. If you keep valuable rewards scarce, you will preserve their value as training tools.

Intermittent rewards

Let's go back to the earlier example of your dog staring at a bird instead of coming to you to go inside. After this incident, you decide to make the effort to train your dog around birds so he can learn to come to you even when birds are around. You set him up far enough away from the bird that he is willing to leave the bird to come to you when you call. Instead of immediately making him come inside when he gets to you, a quick and powerful reward you could immediately use for that awesome recall is to sometimes let him go back and hunt up the bird again! Even better, as soon as he comes to you, you could run back to the tree with him and stand there with him while he looks for a few moments to simulate hunting the bird together. Then you could quietly get hold of him and take him inside. What a thrill that would be for him! That type of reward for coming to you would be far more valuable to him than any treat you could offer and certainly more valuable than going inside where all his hunting fun ends. If you throw in a mega-reward like this every once in awhile, your sporting dog will be more likely to come to you every time you call him, even around birds. He will come to you hoping you will take him to go hunting together.

What you are doing in this case is called giving your dog intermittent reinforcement. He will never know for sure if this is the time he goes in (not very rewarding to him) or goes hunting with you (über rewarding for him). If he really values hunting, he will probably come to you in anticipation of being taken hunting. This is the same basic psychology that keeps gamblers gambling; they continue to gamble because every once in awhile they are rewarded with a jackpot. They never know for sure when they will hit the jackpot again, so they keep plugging coins in the machine, in the hopes of hitting it big. Most of the time there is no pay off, but there are just enough random jackpots to keep the gambler playing. To keep your dog "gambling" and doing what you ask, offer him a special reward once in awhile. Keep him guessing when he will earn something special for doing what you ask and you will be able to achieve far more reliable behaviors from your dog. Assuming it's safe and practical to do so, you can turn the very distractions that cause your sporting dog to ignore you in the first place into mega-rewards to use when training.

The type of training rewards he will earn shouldn't be predictable, either. He should only be able to predict that he will get a reward for performing a correct behavior. If you use treats to reward your sporting dog when he is learning a new behavior, you should begin to periodically introduce other types of rewards, including just praise, as he gains fluency with the behavior. This will keep him interested and working hard to obtain his rewards, since he never knows if he is going to earn a super-duper environmental reward, a tasty treat, or a nice-feeling butt scratch for his efforts.

Why go through all this work to identify rewards?

As mentioned above, sporting dogs are excellent at calculating whether or not doing what you ask them to do is worth their time and effort. In general, a dog will engage in behaviors that get him what he wants or needs and will not engage in behaviors that don't get him something he wants or needs. A variety of rewards will let you mix-and-match behaviors and rewards to achieve the best training results. The harder the behavior is for your dog to perform, the more desirable the reward should be for a correct performance. Keep your dog guessing what he will earn for his efforts by varying the rewards you use to keep learned behaviors strong. Taking the time to figure out what your sporting dog wants most in life will ultimately save you time and effort in your training program and keep your dog interested in working with you long after formal training classes end.

Chapter 7

Creating Your Sporting Dog

Training Plan

You can't depend on your eyes when your imagination is out of focus.

~ Mark Twain

Sporting dogs are energetic, faithful, intelligent companions. They are quick learners and creative problem solvers. But frankly, left to their own devices, they can be quite challenging to live with! A bored sporting dog can wreak considerable havoc by chewing on anything within mouth's reach or finding ways to escape from the yard to go "visit" other dogs or people; an untrained one is apt to be an obnoxious social nerd who greets people and dogs alike with jumping, barking, and general craziness. But if you set clear expectations for your dog's behavior and show him how to meet those expectations, he can become a wonderful canine family member who is a true joy to have around. The challenge is to determine exactly what your expectations are, and then decide how you are going to clearly communicate them to your dog through training. Thinking through how you want your dog to behave in your home and how you will teach him to behave appropriately needs to happen long before you ever pick up your leash and treats to start training. A good training plan will help you keep track of what your behavioral goals are for your sporting dog, how you will meet those goals, and any modifications you may need or want to make to those goals as your training progresses.

What do you want to accomplish?

Before you start training your dog, you need to think about how you want him to behave. You should set the rules of your house, teach him what those rules are, and then consistently enforce those rules. Exactly what your rules are is not nearly as important as the fact that you have rules in the first place and that those rules are consistently enforced. The rules need to fit your personal needs, your lifestyle, and your willingness to put the time and effort required into training your dog to follow your rules.

Some rules take longer to teach than others, and you have to commit to the entire training process if you want to be successful in changing your dog's behavior. Inconsistency is probably the biggest roadblock to training success. Let's consider the following example. Some people don't care if their dogs sleep on the furniture, while other people don't want their dogs to even *look* at the furniture, let alone to get on it. If you don't care if your dog sleeps on the couch, staying off the couch is one less thing you have to teach him. But if you want your dog to stay off the couch, you will need to decide how you will teach him to stay off, invest the time and effort to teach him to stay off, and consistently enforce the rule when he forgets. Developing a training plan to teach him to stay off the couch will help your training stay on track.

A training plan will also help you let go of many of the negative emotions you may be experiencing as a result of your sporting dog's inappropriate behaviors. Of course it is frustrating when your dog won't stop jumping on everyone who walks through your front door or when he refuses to come when called in from the back yard. But when your dog misbehaves, always keep in mind that he is *not* trying to be "bad," "spiteful," or "stubborn," he is just being a sporting dog who needs more training to learn how to behave appropriately in your home. Dogs aren't born knowing how we humans expect them to behave in our homes. They are born only knowing how to act like dogs. It is up to you to teach your dog the rules in your home. When you take the time to develop a training plan, you will identify some of the reasons your dog acts like he does and develop ways to teach him to act differently. The inappropriate behavior is still frustrating, but that irritation can now be channeled into personal motivation to work through your plan. By keeping unproductive negative emotions out of the training process, both you and your dog will have a better time training.

Being precise and thorough in defining your behavior rules will help you set up a good training plan. The sooner you decide what your rules are and start teaching them to your dog, the better it will be for both of you. Behaviors are like habits; the longer you engage in a habit, the longer it takes to break that habit. It is the same with a dog's behavior. If you start teaching your dog how you want him to behave when he is a puppy, it will be a lot easier than if you wait until your dog is older to tell him what your rules are, after he has had plenty of practice misbehaving. You can certainly teach an old dog new behavioral rules, but the older dog may take longer to learn the new rules than a puppy would. Ideally, decide what the rules will be before you even bring your puppy home so you can start teaching him exactly how you want him to behave in your home right from the start. You may need or want to make small adjustments to the rules as time goes on, but defining a clear starting point for your training with a training plan will help you be consistent with his training.

The earlier Doris decides how she would like Keeper to behave in her home, the easier it will be for Keeper to learn the house rules.

Think about all aspects of life with your dog when deciding what your rules will be. What do you want your dog to do when you come to a doorway? What do you want him to do when you put his food bowl down? How quickly do you want him to move when you call him inside from the yard? Where will he sleep? What side do you want him to walk on when you are out together? The earlier you define your rules, the sooner you can start teaching them to your dog.

Let's put this in practice by developing a training plan for teaching your dog to stay off the furniture. When you create your behavior rules, be as black-and-white as you can, because dogs don't understand "shades of gray," or exceptions to rules, very well.

Black-and-white rule: "My dog will not be allowed on the furniture." This is useful because it is very clear cut; the dog isn't going to be allowed on the furniture, period. It will be easy for the dog to understand the rule. When he is physically on the floor, he is behaving correctly. When he jumps up on anything in the room, he is not behaving correctly.

Gray rule: "My dog should stay off the furniture, except for during the day when I'm at work. Then he can lie on the couch and look out the window. But when it's muddy outside, I want him to stay on the floor while I'm gone." This isn't nearly as useful as the previous rule, because you expect your dog to understand that when he has muddy paws, jumping on the furniture isn't allowed. Although sporting dogs are very smart, they aren't smart enough to understand the distinction in behaviors you've just created. Your dog has no way of understanding that because you want to keep your furniture clean, he can't jump on the couch when it rains.

If you are creating new rules for an older dog who has already learned to behave in ways you now want to change, start by creating your new rule, as above. Then identify in as much detail as possible why your dog behaves the way he does right now. This will help you decide how best to change the behavior. Keep in mind that your dog doesn't think about situations in the same way that you do. A dog thinks in rather black-and-white terms about situations—either a particular behavior works to get the dog what he wants or it doesn't work. A sporting dog's environment is full of very rewarding things (we identified many of those environmental rewards in Chapter 6), so if you can identify what your dog gains from his environment by behaving in a certain way, you can use that information to develop an effective training plan to change that behavior.

Useful analysis: "My dog jumps on the couch with muddy feet to watch the rabbits in the front yard. He lies comfortably on the couch to watch them out the window. Sporting dogs instinctively watch things that move. He doesn't understand that his muddy feet are ruining the couch. I have not yet taught him that he must stay off the furniture at all times." This analysis is unemotional and detailed. The likely motivation behind your dog's desire to get on the couch all the time is identified, and makes sense based on basic sporting dog instincts. This analysis also puts the responsibility for the behavior where it ultimately belongs—on you, for allowing your dog to get on the couch in the past, rather than your dog, who was simply doing something you allowed him to do.

Not-so-useful analysis: "My dog knows he should stay off the couch when his feet are muddy. When I yell at him, he looks guilty, so I know he knows he shouldn't be up there. I don't care if he's up there when his feet are clean, but he's really making me angry by getting mud all over the furniture." This analysis places all the responsibility for keeping your couch clean on your dog, even though it is unrealistic to expect him to be able to figure out when he can and when he can't be on the couch (or even what the concept of a "clean" couch is, for that matter). Imputing "guilt" to your dog is also not productive. If you look and sound angry at *any* dog who has appropriate social skills, that dog will start to throw calming signals to try to defuse the situation, even though he may have done absolutely *nothing* to merit any corrections from you! These calming signals (for example, a lowered head and body, lip licking, and tail tucking) can be misinterpreted as the human emotion we call "guilt."

You also need to decide what you would like your dog to do in place of the behavior you are trying to change. This will be the behavior you will actually teach your dog. You've decided you aren't going to allow your sporting dog on your furniture; now you need to decide what you would like him to do instead of hopping up on the couch. The more specific you are about this new behavior, the easier it will be to set up your training plan.

Black-and-white behavior description: "I want my dog to lie on the dog bed beside the couch." This is a very specific behavior that will be easy for your dog to understand and one that you can teach in a step-by-step manner.

Gray behavior description: "I don't care what he does, as long as he stays off my furniture." While this may seem like a precise description of what you want your dog to do, it is actually only a description of what you *don't* want your dog to do. Does this rule mean your dog can do *anything* except jump on the couch? What about getting up on the chairs? Can he run around and pester you when you are on the couch? How exactly will you teach him this rule? You can certainly prevent your sporting dog from getting on the couch through careful management alone, but it is more productive to give him a very precise alternative behavior to learn in addition to managing his behavior.

So far, you have established a behavioral rule for the furniture, and, for the older dog that you want to retrain, identified why he is getting on the furniture in the first place. You've also figured out what alternative behavior you want to teach him. Before you go any further, share this rule with everyone else who has regular interactions with your dog. It is important that your family understands this rule and everyone old enough to understand the rule is willing to enforce it. Consistency is very important in dog training; if one family member allows the dog up on the furniture at the same time you are trying to teach him to stay off the furniture, it will confuse your dog and slow your training progress considerably.

How will you get there?

Once you know what you want to teach your dog, you can decide what combination of management and training techniques you need to use to accomplish that training. In Chapter 5, we looked at why it is important to incorporate management techniques into any training plan when you are trying to change an existing behavior. So while you are teaching your dog to stay off the furniture, you also need to be sure that you find a way to keep him off the furniture between training sessions. Let's assume you already know the primary reason he jumps up on the couch is so he can look out the window at rabbits in the yard. If he couldn't see the rabbits when he climbed up on the couch, he might not try to get on it as often. So preventing your dog from seeing the wildlife in the front yard could be an important management step to use in conjunction with actually training him to lie down someplace other than the couch.

So how you are going to manage the situation? You can: 1) find a way to keep all the rabbits out of your yard; 2) block your dog's view out the window if he does get on the couch; or 3) physically keep your dog from getting up on the couch in the first place. The first option isn't really practical, but blocking your sporting dog's view out the window when he gets on the couch can be accomplished by closing the blinds and curtains on that window when your dog is in that room. However, since the average sporting dog is a creative problem solver, he will most likely quickly figure out a way to scoot the window coverings around so he can still peek out the window. Rearranging the furniture so the couch isn't by the window anymore (at least until your training is done) might also be necessary to keep him from looking out the window. If these two management techniques aren't possible or realistic for you to follow, then you need to physically prevent your dog from getting on the couch. The easiest way to do that is to keep him out of the room with the couch unless someone is there to watch him and keep him off the furniture. If it isn't possible to close a door to that room to keep him out, then confining him in another area of the house that you can block off might work better. Alternatively, using a crate for short periods of time might also work. Another management technique for when you are home would be to tether your dog to you by his leash if you don't have time to keep him off the couch. Simply loop one end of his leash through your belt loop and attach the other end to his collar; this will allow you to go about your business while forcing your dog to stay with you. Now you will know where your dog is at all times, and unless you are sitting on the couch, it is impossible for your dog to get on the couch, because he is tethered to you.

In addition to management, you also need to decide how you will actually teach your sporting dog the new alternative behavior you would like him to do. In our example, your dog is going to be taught to lie down on his dog bed instead of the couch. To create your training plan, start by breaking the behavior down into its components and think about how you will teach your dog each component. Lying in his dog bed instead of on the couch requires your dog to understand several things: he must know how to lie down on cue; he must know how to lie down and stay on his bed. He must know how to go to his bed to lie down instead of climbing up on the couch to lie down. Remember the four stages of learning? First, you need to help your dog acquire an understanding of the new behavior components and then develop fluency in each one. By breaking the behavior you want to teach into its components, you can train in small steps. This will help your dog acquire new knowledge and develop fluency in an efficient way. If you try to go too far, too fast with the training, your dog will get confused and your training will end up taking longer than it would have taken if you had approached the process in small pieces. The management and training exercises in this book are all explained step-by-step to help you understand how to break behaviors down into manageable components to train. Once your dog understands the individual components, you can start to combine them into the final behavior you are working on. There are many books, DVDs, and websites that will help you develop a plan to train behaviors not covered in this book if you don't have access to local training classes.

Don't be afraid to rethink your plan if your training doesn't seem to be going well. Sometimes a training plan that looks perfect on paper doesn't work very well in practice. Adjust as you go along if you need to, but keep the final behavior you want in mind as you adjust your plan. You might decide to change some rules, too. Just remember, if you change the rule later, it will take time for your dog to learn the new rule; expect him to be confused and try to follow the old rule for awhile.

If you are teaching your dog a behavior that he will perform away from home or under varying conditions, you next need to decide how you will generalize this new behavior you've taught your dog so he will perform it any time, any place you ask him to perform it. Once your dog understands the new behavior you are working on, practice it in as many places as possible (if appropriate) with as many different types of distractions as possible so the behavior becomes generalized. Make sure you practice under conditions that are particularly important to you. Dogs don't generalize easily. If you teach your dog to lie on his dog bed when you are sitting on the couch, he won't automatically understand that he must also lie on the dog bed when the kids are sitting on the couch or when guests are over. If you want your sporting dog to lie on his bed when the kids are on the couch or guests are over, then you must train with children and guests around to help him generalize the rule.

The last thing you need to consider is how to maintain the new behavior for your sporting dog's life. Use it or lose it—if you train your sporting dog to lie on his dog bed, but then continue to allow him on the couch every times he tries to get on it, he will quickly start climbing up on the couch again.

Creating your distraction list

Another very important part of your training plan is your distraction list. If you already identified environmental rewards you can use when you are training, you already have a good start on your distraction list! If something is interesting enough to be used as a reward, it is also interesting enough to potentially distract your dog during training. Sporting dogs seem to notice the most insignificant of things sometimes—a leaf blowing in the wind, a spot of dirt on the sidewalk, a tiny crumb of dog treat on the floor. These are the types of things that you may eventually need to train your dog around once he understands the way you expect him to behave, if you want his behavior to become truly reliable.

To make your list, be as specific as possible when you identify distractions. This will let you precisely tailor your training to address distractions that are most important to you and your dog.

Useful distraction description: "My dog is distracted by men wearing baseball caps, small children who are running, and women with long hair." This description of human distractions is useful because it is very specific. You know exactly the type of people you need to make a special effort to include in your training plan.

Not-so-useful distraction description: "My dog is distracted by people." The world is full of all sorts of people. Chances are, if you really pay attention to your dog, he is more distracted by some types of people than others. Dogs are fantastic environmental discriminators and they see differences between many things that we humans tend to miss. If your sporting dog ignores women with short hair but goes berserk around women with long hair, it doesn't really help his training much if you only train around women with short hair. He needs to learn how to behave around women with long hair and the only way to do that is to incorporate women with long hair into your training plan. So the more specific you get with identifying distractions, the more useful that information will be while you are training.

Once you identify something as a potential distraction (you know it's a distraction because your dogs is already paying attention to it), you should rank just how distracting that thing is to your dog. One way to rank distractions is to use a scale from one to ten. If you were to be around the distraction ten times, how many of those times would your dog pay attention to the distraction instead of you? If your dog would perhaps pay attention to the distraction one time out of ten, then you would rate that distraction a one. This is a good distraction to use when your dog is first learning a new behavior. If your dog would pay attention to the distraction ten times out of ten, then you would rate that distraction as a ten. This is one you would save to use later in your training, once your dog is very fluent in the behavior you are teaching and he's started to generalize the behavior.

Write it all down

By developing a training plan, you will be better able to stick to your sporting dog's training, troubleshoot training problems when they arise, and prioritize what you want to teach your dog. But if you are like most people, keeping track of all this information in your head isn't likely to happen. Taking the time to jot down your rules, the behaviors you want to teach, management ideas, and training plans is time well invested in your dog. Your training book doesn't have to be fancy. There is no one perfect format. The book is a tool for *you*, so you need to write information in a way that makes sense to you. If you take the time to write down your plans, you are more likely to follow through with them. Remember, you will probably live with your dog for twelve years or more—the few minutes it takes to write your plan is a very tiny portion of the total time you will live with your dog, but will have a huge impact on the quality of life you have with him for years to come!

It is also ideal that you write down the specifics of each training session so you can assess your dog's training progress. Keeping track of where you practiced, what you practiced, how many times you repeated a behavior, how many times your dog was successful, distractions during your training, and any other information that will help you adjust your training plan is really worth the time it takes. Again, you are the one using the information, so write it down in a way that makes sense to you. And don't give up on training if you forget to write your session information down or you just can't bring yourself to be that analytical; it isn't the end of the world if you don't record all the details of each training session. But the more details you *do* record, the more effective and efficient your training will become. It is definitely time well spent, and it is also a meaningful record of the journey you and your dog take together while training.

15 OCTOBER 2013

BEHAVIOR: SIT

TRAINING LOCATION: AT PARK BY LAKE

DISTRACTIONS USED: DUCKS AND GEESE

SUCCESSFUL REPETITIONS: 2/5

NOTES: BARNUM IS STRUGGLING TO IGNORE BIRDS ON THE LAKE WHEN HE SITS WITH HIS BACK TO THEM. NEED TO PRACTICE SOME MORE HERE, AND ANGLE BARNUM A LITTLE TOWARD THE LAKE FOR THE FIRST FEW SITS TO HELP HIM GET USED TO THE DUCKS BEHIND HIM, BEFORE ASKING HIM TO SIT WITH HIS BACK COMPLETELY TOWARD THEM. ALSO WOULD HELP TO LET HIM LOOK AT THE BIRDS FOR A FEW SECONDS BEFORE ASKING HIM TO TURN HIS BACK ON THEM. JACKPOT HIM THE FIRST TIME HE MANAGES TO SIT STILL WITH HIS BACK TO BIRDS!!

It doesn't matter what format you use, as long as your training records make sense to you and provide you the information you need to move forward with your dog's training.

Training like a sporting dog

Training a sporting dog requires you to be just as focused, enthusiastic, and creative as your dog. Decide how you want your dog to behave, and then actually *do* the training to teach him how to behave. It may seem silly to point out in a training book that it is necessary to actually train your dog, but the truth is, most people want a well-behaved dog, but few are willing to put enough time and effort into training to accomplish that canine transformation. Be consistent and persistent with your expectations when you train. Be patient and exhibit the same level of self-control you expect from your dog; some behaviors take longer than others to teach or modify. Most Americans are formally educated for at least thirteen years to learn all the skills and societal rules we typically need to minimally succeed in our society. Why would we expect our sporting dogs to learn in only one or two training classes all the behaviors he needs to succeed in our world? The more instinctive a behavior is, the longer it will probably take to permanently modify that behavior. Don't set a definite timeline for your training; instead, set a proficiency goal. That way you won't get discouraged if it takes awhile to accomplish some of your training goals. Enjoy the journey you will be taking with your dog instead of focusing on the destination. Before you know it, you will have a well-behaved canine companion who understands the rules of your home!

Chapter 8

Exercise, Exercise, Exercise!

If your dog is fat, you're not getting enough exercise.

~ Unknown

The amount of exercise the typical sporting dog needs is phenomenal. These breeds were developed to help hunters during a time when the dog's ability to hunt mile after mile, day after day, was often relied upon to help put meat on the family dinner table. Before moving on to specific training exercises for sporting dogs, let's take a quick look at the role of physical exercise in the lives of these dogs. Our sporting dogs come from a long line of dogs bred to hunt, run, swim, and carry things on a daily basis; they have an innate need to be physically active. If we don't provide structured ways for our dogs to satisfy this need, they *will* come up with their own exercise activities and the chances are very good that we won't like what they come up with! Too often, the role physical exercise plays in modifying a dog's behavior is overlooked. A well-exercised dog is healthier and better able to focus on learning than a dog who is ready to explode because he's been cooped up in the house all day and has tons of pent up energy to burn. There are many great ways to give your sporting dog adequate exercise and by doing so you will put him in a better frame of mind to get on with the business of learning.

A critical aspect of any dog's overall health is his weight. A seemingly disproportionate number of sporting dogs are overweight by current veterinary standards. Being overweight puts unnecessary extra stress on hips and elbows, which is particularly concerning for breeds prone to hip dysplasia. Keeping your sporting dog at a healthy weight won't guarantee he will never become arthritic or dysplastic, but it does make it easier for him to remain mobile if he does, because he won't be carrying around excess weight. Breeds developed primarily to work in cold water tend to store more fat, which serves as an insulative layer to protect their vital organs from getting too cold while the dogs work in frigid waters, but that doesn't mean that these dogs should ever be "fat." As sporting dogs age, it becomes even more important to keep them at a healthy weight; many dogs will naturally put on excess weight as they become less active with age and their metabolisms begin to slow. This is also the point in their lives when arthritic joint changes begin to develop. Be sure to consult with your veterinarian as your dog ages for advice on proper weight and nutrition for him. A healthy sporting dog is muscular, can move with ease, and often you see at least a slight tuck (the dog equivalent of a waist) and can readily feel his ribs without putting much pressure on his rib cage, even on Labs and other squarer-built breeds. If your dog has no waist at all, can't sustain a trot for very long without becoming winded, or has difficulty standing up and lying down, consult with your veterinarian to develop a plan to get him to a healthier weight and to check for any other health issues. There are many reliable online veterinary resources to help you talk with your veterinarian about your dog's weight. A fat dog is not a sign of a loved dog; he is a sign of a dog whose life is potentially being prematurely shortened by the extra weight he is being forced to carry around.

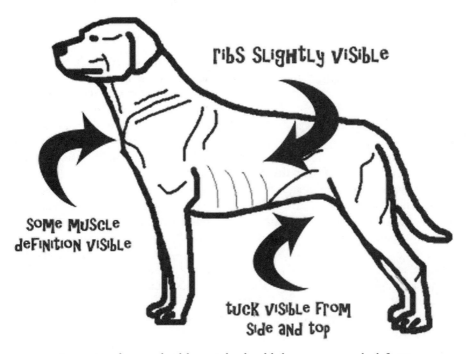

A sporting dog at a healthy weight should show some muscle definition, ribs should be relatively easy to feel, and a tuck should be apparent when looking at the dog from the side and from the top.

Sporting dog-friendly exercise activities

Providing adequate physical exercise for a sporting dog can prove to be a challenge for busy dog owners, but it is absolutely necessary for his mental and physical well-being. Potential dog owners who can't or won't make the commitment to exercising a dog every day shouldn't get a dog who needs a lot of exercise to be healthy and happy. In fact, they probably shouldn't get a dog at all. There are other choices of pets that would be more appropriate for people with sedentary or chaotic lifestyles. A tank of beautiful fish or a small songbird would be a better pet choice than a dog who needs daily vigorous exercise.

When a sporting dog doesn't get enough exercise, he may resort to barking, digging, jumping, chewing, and nipping to help him burn off his excess energy. These are all issues which can make training a dog more challenging than necessary. While you may think that taking a brisk walk around the block twice a day or letting your dog out into the backyard to "run around" by himself is adequate exercise, it doesn't provide anywhere close to the same amount of exercise as running him for miles and letting him swim or retrieve bumpers does. Even having two or more dogs doesn't eliminate the need to provide organized exercise, since most adult sporting dogs only play together in short spurts on their own. Daily vigorous exercise is just as important as food, water, shelter, veterinary care, training, and love to the overall health of your dog. With regular exercise, most people notice a decrease in many of their dogs' behavioral problems. A tired sporting dog is far from a perfect sporting dog, but he is certainly a happier dog who will be much easier to live with and train.

A healthy sporting dog at proper weight can easily run *at least* one mile twice a day and still have plenty of energy left over to train, play, and keep up with the family. The longer-legged, bigger sporting dogs can easily handle two or three miles. *Continuous physical exertion* is the important concept here. Walking a few miles or even allowing the dog to do stop-and-start running off-leash doesn't produce the same physical effects that running at a consistent speed for a significant period of time will produce. Walking is certainly better than no exercise at all, but consider other options to give your sporting dog adequate exercise, if at all possible. Jogging is a far more effective exercise option than walking. Biking is also a great option for many people; using a bike attachment such as a Springer® will allow you to safely bike with your dog without holding on to his leash. Stair walking, both up and down, is good exercise, particularly if you have access to long flights of stairs, such as those found in a sports stadium. Walking in sand, water, snow, or through heavy vegetation will help increase the physical exertion your dog will need to make; even though his speed will be slower if he is walking than if he is running, creating more resistance as he walks will provide him more exercise than merely walking down the sidewalk at a leisurely pace. With proper training, scootering, canicross, skijoring, and even canine treadmill work are also great exercise options.

*Wies keeps her Flat-Coated Retrievers Misty and Denzel
exercised by jogging with them on a daily basis.*

In warmer weather, swimming or running through water will quickly wear a sporting dog out. But never assume that just because you own a sporting breed that traditionally was used to retrieve birds from the water that he knows how to swim! Always start slowly and carefully, walking with your dog in shallow water on leash, gradually increasing the depth until he just loses contact with the bottom. If in doubt, put a dog life jacket on him if you think he might not really understand how to swim yet. And be cautious about trying to "save" a dog if he gets in trouble in the water; a panicked dog poses a very real drowning threat to a human swimmer. Life jackets and long lines are the safest way to help your dog get comfortable in the water and help him if he gets in trouble. Even if your dog doesn't actually swim, tossing toys that will float into shallow water for him to retrieve will increase the amount of exercise your dog gets because running through the shallow water will be more difficult than running on dry land. Just make sure there aren't sharp rocks, broken glass, or other hazards in the water that could hurt your dog. Teaching your dog to swim and retrieve from the water will tap into his natural retrieving instincts while at the same time giving him a good workout that doesn't put a lot of stress on his joints.

Although Wesley probably doesn't need the swim goggles, the life jacket is a wise safety precaution while he learns to swim.

In cold weather, a brief romp through snow drifts will do the trick to get some additional exercise out of your time outside together. Playing fast games of retrieve, especially if the dog has to run uphill to fetch his toy, is good as long as you keep your dog moving. A horse lunge whip with a fuzzy toy or tennis ball tied to the end makes a great chase toy. Just be sure that you run your dog in large circles in both directions when you play and allow him to occasionally catch and play with the toy he has been chasing. If he never gets the chance to catch the toy, he may simply give up chasing it.

There are also a number of competitive dog sports you can participate in that will help you keep your dog exercised and healthy. Agility, tracking, field trials, hunt tests, dock diving, competitive obedience, and competitive canicross are just a few of the dog sports that require routine physically demanding training. Even if you never actually compete, training in one or more of these sports will help you develop a good working relationship with your dog, meet other dog owners who share a similar interest in the sport, and keep both you and your dog moving!

Jeff and Shocker spent countless hours training and exercising together during the years they competed in agility.

Be sure to consult your veterinarian before starting any exercise plan, start slowly, and gradually build up the amount of exercise you give your dog each day. And don't forget to check with your doctor before taking up vigorous exercise with your dog to be sure *you* are up to the challenge as well. Both you and your dog will benefit from making a commitment to daily exercise!

Chapter 9

Management and Training for Lack of Self-Control (Excessive joie de vivre) and Close Bonding with People

---

The hunting partnership between man and dog developed thousands of years ago and from it came a deep bond of affection. I suspect this was the dog's idea.

- Aaron Fraser Pass
American hunting advocate

Sporting dogs, in general, are extroverts. Most are quite friendly with other dogs, sometimes to the point of being socially inappropriate. There are two problems arising from this trait: 1) when your dog gets overly excited about seeing another dog, his adrenaline starts flowing and his ability to think and respond appropriately to your cues starts to decrease; and 2) the dog on the receiving end of your dog's social advances might *not* be friendly, or may simply not want his space invaded by a strange dog. This could escalate into a fight that is actually started by the "friendly" sporting dog who breached social decorum with his inappropriate advances. An ounce of prevention is worth ten pounds of cure when it comes to keeping sporting dogs out of trouble, so we begin with several management techniques to minimize the chances your sporting dog will get over-stimulated or make a fool of himself around another dog.

Most sporting dogs also have a very strong desire to work with and be near their human pack. Patience is a virtue many lack when it comes to interacting with people. Learning to be socially appropriate with people is even more important than learning to be socially appropriate with other dogs. It doesn't matter if your dog was trying to attack or trying to be friendly when he jumps on a person, knocks him down, and breaks his arm. Being out of control around people can be quite dangerous.

This chapter contains many management techniques and training exercises to help your dog develop more self-control. Remember, management techniques don't actually teach your dog *how to* behave, but they can prevent many problem behaviors from happening in the first place and are an important part of sporting dog-centric training. The training exercises will actually *teach* your dog to have more self-control, even in exciting situations, by giving the dog more appropriate, alternative behaviors to perform. Many of the problematic behaviors sporting dogs exhibit, like jumping up, uncontrolled exuberance and the like, can be addressed by helping your dog develop more self-control.

Management techniques

Respect the bubble

Preventing your dog from losing self-control can be accomplished by protecting your dog's personal space. An easy way to visualize your dog's personal space is to imagine him moving through his environment encased in a bubble. The size of the bubble represents the amount of space he needs between him and something exciting or threatening to remain calm and under control. Birds, rabbits, and other small animals, as well as other dogs and people, are all examples of things you may encounter that may overly excite your dog if they get too close to him. If his bubble is intact, he can ignore the distraction, listen to you, and behave appropriately. But if his bubble is popped because the distraction gets too close, your dog stops responding to your cues and starts to lose control. Respecting the bubble is the easiest way to reduce and, in some cases, eliminate many problem behaviors your sporting dog may display out in public and gives you a starting point for actually teaching him more appropriate behaviors.

Bubbles can and do change size depending on past experiences, the type of distraction present, and the amount of training he has received around a particular distraction. The goal of managing your dog's bubbles is to prevent outbursts in the first place. Over time, you can make all the bubbles as small as possible by teaching your dog to pay attention to you even when you are near distractions.

As a puppy, Titus has a very large bubble for just about everything he finds interesting and, as a result, he needs a lot of management to keep his attention focused.

A simple way to identify your dog's bubble size around different distractions is to simply take a few information-gathering walks with him. These walks are not training walks per se; your goal on these walks is to determine how much distance your dog needs between him and various distractions to remain calm in the presence of things that excite him. Pay close attention to all the things that catch your dog's attention and note how close you are when he first starts focusing on them. Identify your dog's bubbles in training classes, at the vet's office, and anywhere else you go with him. If he gets excited and tunes you out at home, identify his home bubbles as well. Make a quick list of these bubbles that you can refer to in the future if you need a reminder. This list will also serve as a yardstick to measure the progress you make in shrinking the bubbles as you begin training. Your goal is to shrink all of your dog's bubbles as much as possible so your dog will listen and pay attention to you even if distractions are nearby. While your dog may always be excited by birds that land a few feet away from him, walking in the park with a dog who wants to go after birds that are 100 yards away will be a miserable experience for both him and you. Identifying your dog's bubbles is the first step in helping him behave more appropriately around distractions.

The goal is to shrink your dog's bubble as much as possible. While he may always react to birds a few feet away, walking in a park with a dog who wants to go after birds 100 yards away will be miserable for you.

Defensive doggie driving

Once you've identified your dog's various bubbles, you need to start practicing defensive doggie driving to protect them. When you take your dog out for walk, the largest bubble you've identified will determine how far ahead you need to proactively scan the environment for distractions. If your dog gets over-the-top goofy about approaching dogs when they are still two blocks away from you, and that is his largest bubble, you need to be scanning proactively at least *three* blocks ahead for other dogs moving toward you. This will give you time to see an approaching dog, decide what you need to do to protect your dog's bubble, and actually start to do it—all *before* your dog's two block bubble is burst and he starts going bonkers, trying to get to the other dog. This is a habit that takes time to develop; most people don't look very far ahead when they walk. Think of proactive scanning as being similar to good defensive driving techniques. You need to walk with your head up, looking forward and scanning the environment as you walk, just as you look ahead and scan when you are driving your car. An added benefit of looking further ahead when you walk is you will appear to walk with more confidence. Dogs are masters at reading body language and when you walk looking ahead of you, your sporting dog will have more confidence in you as his leader. If you look at your feet when you walk instead of out ahead of you, you will appear to lack confidence and you will have no way to effectively protect your dog's bubble from dogs or anything else that gets him aroused because you won't see what's ahead in time to react appropriately.

Kaija is moving briskly confidently, scanning ahead for anything that might cause concern for Bonnie and Clyde.

Defensive doggie driving doesn't just apply when you are out for a walk. When you take your dog into a training class or the vet's office, keep your dog's leash short and your eyes looking ahead. Scan the room before entering and determine where the best place to go with your dog is located. Walk with confidence into the room and go immediately to the spot you pick out. You might not be able to find all the space you would like to have in these situations, but you will certainly help your dog's behavior by picking the best option available to you and confidently filling that space with you and your dog.

Right-of-way rules
Sidewalks are the bane of many a dog owner's existence. Those straight, smooth concrete lines seem to suck all the common sense out of dog walkers when it comes

to preventing unpleasant or uncontrolled encounters between leashed dogs. Canine social rules encourage dogs to approach one another in an arcing manner, body soft, eyes often averted, checking one another out by sniffing rear ends before assessing each other head on. But sidewalks, leashes, and owners prevent this from happening. We humans often stick to that straight sliver of concrete, forcing dogs to approach each other head on, allowing them to strain against their leashes to get to each other, preventing the dogs from doing anything remotely resembling a proper canine greeting ritual. Dogs will often get overly excited or become scared in these situations, leading to confrontations that could be completely avoided if one (or both) dog owners would simply give the right-of-way to the other dog by taking his dog off the sidewalk and moving as far away as necessary to proactively protect his own dog's bubble. This might seem like an obvious thing to do, but few people take this simple step to prevent outbursts from happening in the first place.

Although it might be difficult to remember to yield the right-of-way to distractions at first, once you see how many embarrassing meetings you prevent with this simple technique, you will become motivated to make these adjustments to your walking routine. If there is a dog in the neighborhood who gets your dog excited by running along the fence as you walk, walk on the other side of the street when you pass that house, or take a different route altogether until you have taught your sporting dog to ignore the dog behind the fence. If your dog struggles with calmly passing other dogs head-on, cross the street, or make an about-turn and go back in the direction you came from, or step into the parking strip and have your dog remain stationary near you while the other dog passes, instead of forcing a head-on confrontation between your dog and another dog. If rabbits are known to hide in bushes along a person's driveway and your sporting dog goes crazy trying to hunt them as you walk past, keep your dog away from the bushes in the first place by shortening up his leash and arcing away from the bushes so he can't physically reach them. As you teach your sporting dog how to remain calmer around these distractions and his bubbles start to shrink through training, you won't need to make as many detours in your walking path. But until your dog learns new coping skills, walk the few extra steps it takes to yield the right-of-way and keep your dog out of the path of oncoming trouble, pat yourself on the back for being a responsible, proactive dog owner, and remind yourself you've also just added a few extra steps to your dog's daily exercise quota as a bonus!

When you alter your path to avoid distractions, turn with confidence and authority, then step out at a brisk pace in your new direction. Talk to your dog in a pleasant, calm tone as you walk away. If your dog likes treats, offer him a few as you walk away, but only if he is going with you and not straining to turn back to the distraction. You want to reward walking away with you, not looking back at the distraction. Don't nag your dog or yell at him if he keeps turning around. If he reacts to the distraction at all, it is a sign that *you* waited too long to try to avoid the situation and his bubble was burst. Just continue to walk away with confidence. Eventually there will be enough distance between your sporting dog and the distraction to allow him to regain his composure. Distance is always your friend. You will never go wrong if you calmly and promptly increase the distance between your dog and anything that arouses him as a way to help him remain calm.

Ideally, if your timing is good and you scan proactively far enough ahead on your walk, your dog should not be distressed by the sudden change in your walking route. The key with this technique is to be confident in your body language and voice as you change direction. Your dog is a master at reading body language and will pick up on any tenseness in your body or voice. If you display tension, it will make your dog even more excited or worried about the oncoming distraction. In his mind, he might associate the distraction with your tension (which in this case would be correct!). But if you act unconcerned and nonchalant about the distraction as you move away, your confidence will help your dog move away from the distraction more calmly, too.

Keep calm and move on

At the outbreak of World War II, the British Ministry of Information created motivational posters to bolster British morale if the Germans ever invaded the island. One poster carried the simple slogan "Keep calm and carry on." You can certainly make good use of this slogan today in your dog training. Sometimes you have no choice but to walk close to something that will get your sporting dog overly excited. Sometimes your dog will see a bunny before you do. Sometimes you will encounter something new with your dog and he will have an unexpected initial reaction to it. Sometimes life happens in spite of your best intentions and your dog's bubble is burst. When things like this happen and your dog gets aroused or starts acting out, it is very important that you keep calm and move on. It is not always easy to do, but this will minimize the trauma and drama of the situation for both you and your dog.

When something unexpected happens, keep as calm as possible, keep your feet moving, and get your dog out of the situation as quickly as you can!

When a person gets excited or nervous, many physical and physiological changes occur; body posture, breathing patterns, voice tone and inflection, and hormone levels can all change without a person even really being aware of the changes. Dogs are masters at reading these subtle changes when your adrenaline starts flowing. Your dog may respond to these changes in your appearance and behavior, so if you are upset, it is likely your dog will get upset as well once he senses these changes. Although it is impossible to completely fool you dog, you can certainly minimize the impact your emotions have on your dog's behavior by making a conscious effort to keep calm. If your dog's bubble gets burst or something unexpected happens and your dog gets out of control, take a deep breath, straighten your shoulders, stand tall, and then calmly and quickly get your dog out of the situation. Don't yell at your dog or try to reason with him about his behavior—do you really think he understands you when you tell him the other dog doesn't want to play? Keep your voice calm and quiet and keep your feet moving. A quiet voice is often more confident sounding than a loud one. If you maintain a façade of calm authority, it will help you get out of a difficult situation with a minimum of difficulty.

Calming signals
Turid Rugaas, in her book *On Talking Terms with Dogs,* has written extensively about the ways dogs use certain types of body language (called "calming signals") to try to defuse tense situations. You can use some of these same signals to try to calm your dog when he is faced with an exciting situation. Yawning, licking your lips, and avoiding head-on confrontations or direct eye contact are easy behaviors that your dog may recognize you can do that may help calm your dog down.

*Barnum was nervous about having his picture taken
and tried to defuse a stressful situation by yawning.*

Remember that dog behavior is just that—behavior. Dogs aren't human. They don't act out of spite, vengeance, or pre-meditated hostility. Their actions are a very complicated mixture of instincts and environmental learning. When your dog does something that you don't like, consider that behavior to be information. Your dog is constantly trying to tell you exactly what he does and doesn't know, what is distracting to him, what frightens him or excites him, and what he would rather be doing at any particular moment. If you remain calm and pay attention to the information you are being given, you can then tailor your training plan to change the behaviors you want to alter. Once you know how your dog behaves, you need to accept responsibility for taking that information and using it to develop a training plan to help your dog behave more appropriately in the future.

Six feet is a privilege, not a right

Many owners freeze as soon as their dogs start acting up or, even worse, allow their dogs to pull out at the end of a six-foot leash and drag them closer to whatever the dogs want to investigate. When that happens, exactly who is walking whom? From your dog's perspective, pulling is worthwhile because this behavior gets him closer to what he wants to check out. The consequences of his behavior are desirable to him, so it is likely he will continue to pull toward things that excite him in the future. And the further away your dog is from you, the easier it is for him to ignore you when he is excited and the less physical control you have over him. Walking at the end of a six foot of leash is a privilege, not a right, and pulling is never acceptable. When you are moving past distractions that might excite your dog, shorten up that leash and keep your dog close to you. Keep your feet moving and don't slow down as you move past. This will minimize the amount of time your dog has to get excited and ends any potential outburst that much sooner.

Be your dog's advocate

Taking responsibility for your sporting dog's safety and well-being is an important part of being a loving dog owner. Sometimes that responsibility requires you to tell other people (and their dogs) that they can't interact with your dog. When sporting dogs are puppies, they need as much socialization with socially-appropriate dogs of all ages, shapes, sizes, colors, and both sexes as they can get. They need to meet dogs that will play with them and dogs that will tell them (appropriately) to go away. Most sporting dogs really need to learn that "no" means "no" when it comes to social interactions. But not every dog you meet in the neighborhood has the proper social skills to teach your puppy these important lessons. You need to accept responsibility for keeping your sporting dog, whatever his age, out of potentially explosive encounters with dogs he doesn't know.

Too often, an owner of a "friendly" dog will allow his dog to rush up to other dogs he has never met before, calling out "It's OK—he's friendly and just wants to say hi!," assuming the other dog is equally eager to interact. They will do this without giving a thought about whether it is appropriate for that interaction to occur in the first place, or if the other dog owner even wants his dog to be approached. Suzanne Clothier, a well-known dog trainer, wrote a fantastic article a few years ago that discusses the problems that can occur between a dog who "just wants to say hi" and a dog he's never met before. She analogizes the goofy, over-the-top greetings that some dogs dish out to an uncomfortably close encounter between a man and a woman who have never met before. Her article is definitely worth reading. The point of her article is that no person would expect one human to tolerate inappropriate physical contact from another human simply because that other person is "friendly," so why should we expect our dogs to tolerate inappropriate behavior from other dogs simply because an owner says "my dog is friendly"? Whether your sporting dog is the one who prefers his own personal space or the one who is the social nerd who wants to meet every other dog he sees, you must be your dog's advocate and try to prevent these types of "greetings" from happening. If you don't, the odds are really good your dog will end up getting scared or hurt as a result of an inappropriate encounter someday.

To deal proactively with these types of situations, you must never assume a person will control his dog appropriately or see anything wrong with how his dog is acting. If someone asks if his dog can say "hi" to yours, politely decline if you suspect the greeting will cause problems for your dog. Explain that your dog is learning good greeting manners so you need to pass on the meeting; that should deter the other owner from approaching. Unfortunately, some dog owners can't talk and keep their dogs close to them at the same time! Be sure to watch the other dog while this conversation is going on, so the dog doesn't pull too close to yours. Never be afraid to ask another dog owner to call his dog away, either. Even if the owner says "It's OK—my dog's friendly!" that doesn't give the dog the right to assault your dog (nor should *you* say that to someone else and then allow *your* dog to pull over to another dog without permission). The over-exuberant, "friendly" dogs are often the ones that cause the most problems. They may approach head on, choking against their collars, gasping for air, feet flying, and immediately they throw themselves on top of the dogs they are greeting. A normal response for the targeted dog would be to growl, bark, and perhaps even bite the approaching dog to get him to back off. No dog should have to tolerate that type of behavior from another dog. The other dog isn't being mean or aggressive if he reacts this way when he is "attacked with friendliness," he is just reacting to a socially inappropriate situation that never should have happened in the first place.

And of course it is *never* appropriate to allow your dog, no matter how friendly, to run up on a strange dog. It is disrespectful to the other owner and dangerous for both dogs when you assume, because your dog is friendly, everything will be fine. An adult dog, even if he really enjoys interacting with other dogs, should not be desperately trying to get to every other dog he sees. His most pleasant and preferable interactions should be with you. If he is more interested in other dogs than you, you may need to examine your relationship with your dog more closely. Many times we get so wrapped up in our daily lives that the only time we might spend with our dogs is a walk around the block in the evening or letting the dog outside. Sporting dogs crave social interaction, and if they don't get enough from their human pack, they will try to get it from other dogs, whether or not it is appropriate to do so. Giving your dog quality time and attention on a daily basis is a crucial element in helping him demonstrate more self-control around other dogs.

When one or both dogs are attached to a leash, the situation can become even more unpredictable. A leash removes a dog's ability to flee a threatening situation (assuming he wants to run away in the first place), and also hinders his ability to fully communicate with his body, especially when the leash is being held tight by a nervous owner who freezes instead of moving his dog calmly out of a potentially dangerous situation. Always err on the side of caution when allowing two dogs who have never met before to meet one another on leash. You will never cause a problem if you don't allow the two dogs to meet; you just might create a lifelong problem for one or both dogs if something goes wrong during an on-leash meeting.

Being your sporting dog's advocate also applies to choosing places to take your dog. Don't take your dog into a situation you know he isn't ready to handle yet or one you can't manage well enough to prevent him from behaving inappropriately. For example, many pet stores allow you to take leashed pets in with you to shop. The store is full of narrow aisles, limited visibility, and lots of exciting sights and smells. The floors are usually slick and difficult for some dogs to walk on without slipping. Other shoppers are pushing carts and many people assume if a dog is brought into the store, he is friendly with all people and all dogs. This can be a high-stress situation for your dog. Bringing your dog into this type of situation without first teaching him how to successfully cope with that high level of stress is asking for trouble. It would be far more prudent to leave your dog at home when you go out to buy dog food until you have taught your dog how to behave in highly distracting environments. Even if your dog is friendly, he may trigger responses in other dogs in the store if he pulls, jumps, whines, and gags trying to get closer to other dogs.

If your sporting dog doesn't have the skills to cope with a lot of distractions yet, find a quiet park where there usually aren't many dogs or walk around the neighborhood where you are both comfortable, while he is learning how to behave. As you teach your sporting dog behaviors to cope with more stressful environments, you will eventually be able to add more places, like the pet store, into your travels together. But if you repeatedly over-stimulate your dog by putting him in situations he isn't able to handle, you are simply giving him more practice at the very behaviors you want to change. You're also teaching him that he can't really trust you to keep him safe, or that being an over-the-top nerd is appropriate. If you gradually increase the distractions your dog must deal with as he learns how to behave, before long you will end up with a dog that you can take just about anywhere and one that other people would like to have!

Don't strangle the dog!

While this may seem to be a strange management technique, it is a very important one. When a dog gets excited, he usually starts straining against his leash and collar. When this happens, his airflow becomes restricted and his body automatically responds as if he is being choked (because he is!). This will immediately arouse any dog and just adds to the excitement your dog is already feeling. He doesn't understand that *he* is causing the pressure on his neck which is cutting off his air. He thinks that whatever is arousing him (another dog, a bunny) is taking his breath away. This can make him even more reactive toward that type of distraction in the future, even though he might not actually be straining against his collar at the time, because he associates the distraction with the choking sensation.

If you can protect your sporting dog's bubble, you won't have many situations where you dog will pull against his collar in the first place. But for those times when an outburst happens in spite of your best efforts, try to keep some slack in the leash to minimize the pressure on his trachea while you move away from whatever is exciting your dog. One trick you can use if you are walking your dog on a fixed-length leash is to create a quick no-pull harness with the leash to help you maintain physical control over your dog in unexpected situations. Reach over your dog's back. Move the ring that the leash is attached to on his collar toward his chest, so the leash clasp is hanging down between the dog's front legs. Slip the leash between your dog's front legs and out from under his belly on his left side. Hold the leash up at your dog's back level with your left hand and let the handle end of the leash drop back down on the left side of your dog, resulting in a big loop of leash laying against your dog's left side. Pass the handle under your dog's belly and bring it up on his right side with your right hand. Slip the handle under the loop of leash you created on the left side and pull the leash snugly up around your dog's chest. Hold the leash by the handle. If your dog continues to strain against the leash as you walk, this arrangement will put more of the pressure on your dog's chest rather than his windpipe and will help him remain a little calmer, because the choking sensation will be decreased.

You can use your dog's leash to make a quick no-pull harness for emergency situations.

Along with keeping the pressure off your dog's neck when he is excited, try to keep all four of his feet on the ground. If your sporting dog is gasping, crying, and walking on his hind legs as he tries to approach another dog, he will appear very threatening. The other dog doesn't know your dog can't get to him because you are holding his leash; he just sees a canine Frankenstein heading right for him. This can cause the other dog to become excited or scared and the situation can quickly spiral out of control. If you can't keep your dog on the ground, walk in another direction to create more distance between the dogs as quickly as possible.

Keep 'em busy

When you have to stay in a distracting environment with your sporting dog, you may need to keep him busy to keep him calm. This is particularly true in group training classes where your dog must be in close proximity to other dogs for fairly long periods of time. If you don't keep your dog's attention, he will find something to pay attention to on his own, and the odds are pretty good it won't be you. You need to actively engage him to keep him from fixating on distractions in his environment. If you attend group classes, you must focus on your dog from the moment you pull into the parking lot until the moment you leave. Keeping your dog on a very short leash so he is close to you as you enter and leave the training building will help him keep his focus on you. But once you take your seat, you will need to continue to engage your dog so he will pay more attention to you than to other dogs in class what your sporting dog is paying attention to. A sterilized hollow bone filled with peanut butter, wet dog food, or squeezed cheese and then frozen is a great distractor for your dog, as long as he is calm enough to eat. Tricks, basic obedience commands, or a game of hand targeting will also keep your sporting dog focused on you instead of the other dogs in the class;

just be sure your dog's activities aren't too distracting for the other dogs. It is a lot of work to keep a dog focused on you for an entire class, but it is important to prevent him from getting overly excited or getting other dogs overly excited by his antics.

Say what you mean, mean what you say

Many times you may think your dog is being strong-willed or independent when he doesn't behave the way you expect him to behave. But the truth is that poor communication skills are often the cause of the problem. Dogs don't understand human language the same way we do. Consider the phrase "Sit down." If you tell a person to sit down, he would probably understand you want him to assume a seated position. But your dog may respond quite differently to that phrase. If your dog already understands the behaviors you want when you say "Sit" and "Down" separately, he would understand your phrase "Sit down" as a two link behavior chain; first a sit, followed immediately by a down. The end result would be your dog sitting, then lying down. And if you actually wanted him to sit when you said "Sit down," you might think your dog didn't do what you told him to do because he sat, but then laid down. But in reality, your dog did *exactly* what you told him to do. If you wanted him to sit, you should have simply said "Sit."

Another possible response from your dog when you say "Sit down" is that your dog sits. You probably wouldn't think of this as an incorrect response to your cue "Sit down," because *you* know you meant for him to sit. But you actually *told* him to sit and then lie down. When your dog didn't lie down, it means that either your dog doesn't actually understand the down cue yet or, for some reason, he didn't perform the down behavior. Either way, if you don't help your dog lie down, you are teaching him he doesn't need to lie down each and every time he hears "Down," by not enforcing the cue.

Words have very specific meanings to your dog, so you need to be sure you use your training words carefully and consistently to help your dog. Say exactly what you mean, and mean exactly what you say. If you follow that rule, your dog will have an easier time doing what you want him to do. Pick a unique, distinct cue for each behavior you teach him and then use those cues consistently. For example, don't use the cue "Down" to mean lie down in some situations, and to get off of something (like the couch) in other situations. The specific words you use don't really matter; you can teach your dog to come to you when he hears the word "Rutabaga" as easily as when he hears the word "Come." As long as you teach your dog what exact behavior you expect when you say a particular word and are consistently using that word to initiate that one behavior only, your dog will understand what you expect him to do and you will both be much happier!

When the words don't work

No matter how consistent you are with your cues, if you aren't consistent with using and enforcing those cues, they weaken over time. If you want to retrain a weak behavior, it may be quicker and easier to change the word you use for that behavior rather than continuing to use the weak cue word. For example, imagine you own a five-year-old Cocker Spaniel who comes to you when he hears the word "Come" about 25%

of the time because you haven't been consistent in enforcing the recall every time you called him. If he didn't come to you, you didn't help him finish the behavior; you just walked away and eventually he would wander over to you when he felt like doing so. He has a five-year-long history of failing to respond to the word "Come" every time he hears it. Now you decide you want to teach him to come to you each and every time he is called, the very first time you call. You can certainly continue to use the word "Come" and start to consistently enforce the behavior, but it will take quite some time to make a permanent change in your dog's behavior because he already learned his response to that word is optional, as demonstrated by the fact that three times out of four he fails to come when you call him. He will need to "unlearn" the response of ignoring you and "relearn" the response of coming each and every time he hears the word "Come." A faster way to retrain this behavior is to use a completely new cue for it. Instead of continuing to use the word "Come" and dealing with all the practice your dog has had ignoring that cue, start from the beginning teaching a consistent recall with a new cue word, such as "Here" (or any other word you want to use); this is a brand new cue with no history of being ignored attached to it. If you start training your dog to come to you the very first time he hears the word "Here," and consistently reinforce your behavioral expectations with that word, your dog will actually learn to come reliably with this new cue more quickly than he would if you try to retrain the behavior using the old cue "Come." If you want your dog to come every time he is called, it will be up to you to make sure he does come every time you say "Here." If you don't have the time or inclination to reinforce the behavior, then you simply don't use your new recall cue! If your dog is running after a bird in the backyard and you haven't taught him to come to you in the presence of such distractions yet, don't weaken or ruin your new cue by saying "Here!" over and over; if you have to say anything at all, use your old cue ("Come") that is already broken (i.e., he already has a history of ignoring that cue). That way you don't undo any of the training you are doing with the new cue. If you use your new cue when you have no way to enforce it and your dog doesn't perform the desired behavior, you are teaching your dog that this new cue can also be ignored, just like the old cue. It doesn't matter what the particular behavior is; every time you give your dog a cue and then allow him not to perform the behavior, you are actually teaching him that responding to your cue is purely optional.

Protect your cues by using them only when you can help your dog complete the desired behavior if he doesn't do it on his own; if you can't help him, don't give him the cue in the first place. In this way, your words will retain their meaning to your dog and he will be more likely to respond to them reliably. And if a cue is already broken, consider retraining the behavior using a new cue. Your sporting dog will thank you for eliminating a lot of confusion for him!

Training exercises

Now that you have a selection of management techniques to make some quick behavioral fixes, let's look at some training exercises that will actually teach your sporting dog how to behave in situations that may excite him. Remember that thoroughly training any behavior takes time and you will need to gradually increase the intensity of the distractions you train your dog around as your dog develops fluency. To deal with excessive *joie de vivre*, and close bonding to people, you will be training your sporting dog to exhibit a higher degree of self-control than he normally would show if left to make his own choices. You will need to reinforce and strengthen his self-control with rewards that appeal to his instincts, to increase the likelihood that he will exhibit self-control in the future.

If you didn't make your dog's reward list in Chapter 6 and distraction list in Chapter 7, this would be a good time to go back and make those lists before you start training. You will need to use both of them in order to efficiently teach your dog how to exhibit control around things that excite him.

Hand target

Exercise Goal: Your sporting dog will touch your hand with his nose regardless of where you put your hand.

Teaching your dog to focus on your hand and touch it with his nose is a very useful behavior. You can use it to keep your dog busy and focused on you, as well as to move him into different positions quickly and easily and keep him moving right beside you without pulling on his leash. A hand target can also work as a backup recall. If your dog learns to enjoy running to you to hit your hand with his nose, you can use that behavior to get him close to you if he fails to come when you use your recall cue.

Kegan loves to touch Karen's hand to earn a reward, so she can use it as a backup recall cue.

1. Before you start training your dog, find a ruler or measuring tape. Sit it in front of you and put your thumb on the one inch mark and your forefinger on the two inch mark. Without moving your fingers, lift up your hand and look at the space between your fingers. That is how big one inch is. Why is this important to do before you start teaching your dog this behavior? Because you should start this training by holding your

hand no more than one inch from your dog's nose. But most owners cheat and put their hands six inches or more away from their dogs the very first training session, and then get frustrated because their dogs don't do anything. By reminding yourself exactly how big one inch is, you will hopefully not make the same mistake with your dog and will have success with this training right from the start!

2. Start this exercise with your dog on-leash in a quiet, calm environment. Have small, tasty treats available for rewards. Keep the treats in your pocket or in a bowl nearby so your dog won't be distracted by them. Sit or step on the end of the leash so your dog can't decide to walk away while you are training, but be sure to leave enough slack in the leash so he can sit or stand comfortably.

3. For this behavior, it doesn't matter what position your dog is in when you start the training. The way you hold your hand will become the visual cue for this behavior, so it will need to be somewhat unique. Hold the index finger and middle finger of one hand out (as if you are pointing to something with those two fingers), and curl your thumb, ring finger and pinky finger in toward your palm.

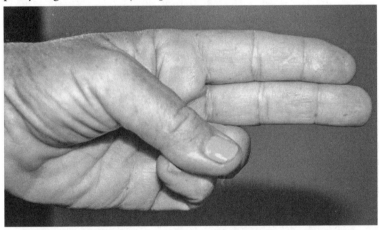

By holding your hand in a specific way, your dog will learn when he should touch your hand and when he should leave it alone.

You will present this visual cue with the back of your hand toward your dog. Hold your hand one inch in front of your dog's nose. Stand still and *be quiet* while your dog figures out what you want him to do—don't wiggle your hand around or nag him. Most dogs will touch your hand out of curiosity (or because your hand smells like treats). As soon as you feel your dog's nose touch your hand, praise and reward him. Don't cheat and move your hand toward your dog—be sure your dog moves toward your hand to touch it. If you can't resist the urge to move your hand toward your dog to help him be successful, don't look at your dog while you are teaching this behavior. Instead, train by feel alone; reward when you feel his nose touch your hand.

4. If your dog doesn't show any interest in your hand within ten seconds, drop your hand to your side and move your dog a few steps away to a new spot and try again. Make sure you are actually holding your hand only one inch from his nose. If something in the environment is distracting your dog, remove the distraction or find a less distracting place to train. If your dog still won't interact with your hand, place a very tiny piece of treat between the extended fingers of your target hand and try again. Your dog should touch your hand to try to get the treat. Repeat this three more times with a treat between your fingers, then immediately repeat without the treat. Your dog should touch your hand in anticipation of getting the treat between your fingers. Quickly praise and give him a treat from your pocket or treat bowl as soon as you feel him touch your hand. If you need to jump start your sporting dog by using a treat between your fingers, get rid of the treat as quickly as you can. If you rely too long on a treat to get your dog to interact with your hand, he will have problems performing the behavior when you take the treat away.

5. Practice with your hand one inch from your dog's nose until he will touch it as soon as you put it in front of him at least 80% of the time. Be sure to practice with both hands. Your dog may not understand that if he performs a behavior on your right side that he can also perform it on your left side unless you help him generalize the behavior by having him touch both your right and left hands. You can also add a verbal cue to the behavior at this point, if you want, by simply saying "Touch" as you feel him touch your hand.

Linda holds her hand one inch away from Maya's nose in the early stages of target training so Maya can be successful.

6. Increase the distance your dog must move to touch your hand by one inch increments, using the 80% rule to help you decide when to add more distance. Once your hand is far enough away that your dog must actually take a step or two to get to it, he may seem a little confused. Up

to this point, he didn't have to move his body much to perform the touch behavior because your hand was so close to him. You have now essentially added another behavior he must do before he can touch your hand. Be patient and *quiet* while he figures out that he needs to move his entire body toward you to touch your hand. Resist the urge to move your hand toward him to "help" him. If he hasn't moved toward your hand within ten seconds, drop your hand to your side, get your dog up and move to a different spot in the room to try again. If he still struggles, decrease the distance between your hand and his nose until he is successful, then start building distance back up from there.

7. Once your dog is walking toward your hand to touch it, you can begin to present your hand in different places relative to your body. Hold it high, low, behind you, and in between your legs. Also practice showing him the target while you are walking with him. Getting him comfortable touching your hand in all different positions and while you are both moving will turn this behavior into a handy training tool for teaching other behaviors. You can also start substituting environmental rewards for treats at this point. For example, ask for a hand touch before you let your dog out into the yard to play. Going outside becomes his reward for performing the hand touch. This is a super easy, quick way to sneak in a little training in the course of everyday activities and it constantly reminds your dog that if he wants something *from* you (like being let outside), he must first do something *for* you (like touch your hand).

Linda gradually increases the distance Maya must move to complete a hand touch until she has to walk to touch Linda's hand.

8. Most dogs enjoy this behavior once they understand what you want. Sometimes they will become quite creative and start touching you even when you don't ask them to touch. If your dog starts experimenting

with the behavior and touching your hand when you haven't asked for a touch, simply ignore him. Don't look at him or say anything to him; just ignore him. This spontaneous behavior will stop if it is never reinforced. He will learn that the only time he should touch your hand is when you are holding your two fingers out and tell him to touch.

This is a particularly fun behavior for young children to do (with adult supervision), once your dog knows what to do. Hold the child's hand in yours and help him put his fingers out, then tell the dog to touch the child's hand. This will help the child learn how to interact with the dog in an appropriate manner using a fairly simple behavior, as well as reinforce to the dog that he must listen to all the members of the family, regardless of their size.

Sporting dog red light/green light

Exercise Goal: Your sporting dog will learn how to regain focus and respond to cues after he has been excited.

Another training exercise that helps build self-control, while at the same time reinforces basic obedience cues, is the sporting dog version of the child's game called Red Light/Green Light. This is an active game that requires you to move around and entice your dog to move around with you, so be sure you have plenty of room to work in. Over time, your dog will learn to quickly shift between working and playing with you. You will also learn how to read his body language better and identify when your dog is on the verge of becoming too excited to respond to you if you play this training game.

1. Start this game with your dog on-leash in a secure area large enough to move around in easily (this is a good game to play in a fenced yard). You will not use treats for this game; your attention and play will be the rewards your dog earns for paying attention to you. Hold on to the leash while you are playing for the first few sessions to be sure your dog won't try to leave you if he gets too excited.

2. The first thing your sporting dog must learn is how to play with you without biting or losing control. You can control most of this through the way you play with him and how long you play together. The rougher the play and the longer the time, the more likely your dog will get overly excited. Start by gently playing with your dog, giving him a few soft pats, talking goofy to him, and generally encouraging him to get a little excited. Pay close attention to his body language. If he seems scared of your motions, slow down a bit. If he starts to get really jazzed and tries to nip, stop the game immediately. Stand absolutely still and silent a few moments, then try to slowly pat your dog again. Most of the time when a dog nips, it is because you've moved too fast with the game and your dog's retrieving (oral) instincts took over (or your dog has been allowed to bite you in the past). If your dog still tries to nip even when you are standing still, give him a firm verbal "no bite," get hold of his leash, and have him do a behavior he knows, such as sit or touch. If he is too excited to listen to you, don't repeat the cue. Instead, help him perform the behavior, then put him in his crate or another room to calm down. Don't put him out in the yard to run around, hunt for birds, and gener-

ally do as he pleases, as most dogs would see this as a reward for their behavior rather than a punishment. It is never acceptable for your dog to use his teeth on you, but the more aroused he becomes, the more difficult it is for him to control his oral instincts and discriminate between your hands and something he can put in his mouth.

Keagan mirrors Karen's excited attitude and posture as they play with each other.

3. After your dog appears to have had time to start calming down, quietly give him his freedom back. Don't make a big silly fuss over him or scold him for getting too rough earlier. Just matter-of-factly let him out, go about your business, and let him go about his. The next time you start this exercise, move slowly and more deliberately until your dog has learned more self-control.

4. Once your dog is getting excited about your play without losing control, you can add in the control part of this game. Play with your dog for a few moments, then stand up straight, quit moving, and in a very calm voice, ask him for a familiar behavior he knows, such as sit. Your body

language and voice should be very calm and quiet compared to your body language and voice when you are playing. If your dog sits, immediately start playing with him again, using inviting body language and a goofy voice to let him know the game is back on! If he doesn't perform the behavior, demonstrate your own self-control by not repeating the command. Instead, gently but matter-of-factly help your dog into a sit. Pet him for a few seconds while he is sitting, then release him and start playing again. For this training, your play is the reward that your dog gets for responding to your cues.

5.   Gradually increase the intensity of your play between behaviors as well as the difficulty of the behaviors you ask from your sporting dog as he begins to understand the rules of the game. Always be sure to stand still and ask for behaviors in a calm, confident voice; your change in body language will be a significant cue to your dog to settle down and listen. Vary the length of time you ask him to hold a position, or ask for a couple of behaviors in rapid succession before resuming play. Your dog should never be able to anticipate what you are going to ask him to do, when you are going to ask him to do it, or how long he will need to keep doing it before being released to play some more with you. The more contrast there is between play and work, the easier it will be for your dog to maintain his self-control when he needs it.

6.   Once you can stop and start your dog when you play with him using only your voice and body, you can start adding in playing tug with a toy. Tug slowly and gently with your dog, then let go of the toy, stand still and ask him to perform a behavior. Don't worry if he doesn't give the toy right back. For this exercise it is OK for him to sit while continuing to hold his toy. Just remember to have either the dog or the toy on a leash while you are playing so your sporting dog can't decide to run away with his toy and stop playing with you. When the game is back on, calmly reach down and get ahold of the toy, then start playing again.

Over time, the body language you use in this game will begin to trigger a predictable response in your dog. If you get into a "game on" stance every time you start to play this game, before long your sporting dog will get excited when you assume that stance, even if you don't follow it with play. Conversely, if you are careful about being very still and calm before you ask your dog to perform a specific behavior, that posture will get your sporting dog more focused and ready to work. Because you always have your body with you, it is well worth your time to play this game and get your dog tuned into these body cues. Then you can use those same cues to get your dog energized or calm him down, as situations warrant. And all without treats!

Note how Karen's calm demeanor is reflected in Keagan's behavior, even though Karen is still holding the tug toy they were playing with moments earlier.

Patience is a virtue

Exercise Goal: Your sporting dog will learn that you control all the resources, including anything you happen to be holding.

This is a classic training game (also commonly referred to as Doggie Zen) for teaching your dog to get what he wants by exhibiting self-control and patience. It can also be used as the foundation for teaching your dog to stay. The most difficult thing for most owners to remember when they play this game is to keep quiet and allow their dogs to figure out how to earn the rewards by themselves.

1. Start this exercise with your dog on-leash in a quiet, calm environment. To help make this exercise easier to learn, have some small ordinary treats available for rewards; it will be easier for your dog to ignore a piece of kibble than it will be to ignore a piece of chicken, so for this exercise, use a fairly boring treat for your first few training sessions. Keep the treats in your pocket or in a bowl nearby so your dog won't be distracted by them. Sit or step on the end of the leash so he can't decide to walk away while you are training. Your dog can be in any position to play this game.

2. Put one treat in the palm of your hand and hold your hand about twelve inches in front of your dog's face. Let your dog see the treat but do *not*

let him take the treat from your hand. If your dog moves to take the treat (and he probably will at first), close your hand over the treat and wait for him to leave your hand alone. Don't say anything. Simply close your hand over the treat and wait for your dog to stop pestering your hand. It is very important that you don't jerk your hand away from him. That type of sudden motion will encourage him to grab your hand or jump up toward you. Hold your hand steady, but close it over the treat if he gets rude and tries to take it from you. He may scratch, bark, and push for quite some time if he is highly food motivated, but eventually he will stop trying to get the treat, even if only for a split second. As soon as he leaves your hand alone, praise and give him the treat. He is learning that if he is polite and patient, you will gladly give him what he wants. Some dogs will simply quit moving toward your hand, others will look at you, and a few will even back away from your hand as they catch on to this game. It doesn't matter what behavior your dog does, as long as he isn't trying to get the treat; if he leaves your hand alone, he has earned his reward. Remain silent during this exercise. If you tell your dog to "leave it" or "no" every time your dog tries to get the treat, you are taking responsibility for your dog showing self-control. But if you allow your dog to experiment and figure out on his own that leaving your hand alone will earn him his treat, he will be more polite of his own free will in the future.

Poppy tries to get the treat out of Dena's hand, but Dena quietly waits, without pulling her hand away, until Poppy stops trying before giving her the treat.

3. As soon as your dog can leave the treat in your hand alone, begin to gradually increase the amount of time your dog must wait before getting his treat. Start out asking for a second of calm behavior while you hold the treat in your open hand. *Any* behavior is acceptable except for pawing, scratching, nosing, or otherwise actively trying to get the treat. If he tries to get the treat, close your hand over the treat until he settles down again. When your dog can ignore the treat for one second 80% of

the time (four out of five times), ask for two seconds of calm behavior before praising and delivering the treat. Gradually increase the amount of time he must remain calm to get his treat, always keeping in mind the 80% rule when you want to make the exercise more difficult. Eventually you will find that your dog will start relaxing and possibly even looking at you while he waits for his treat. If you are consistent with the rules of the game, he will soon learn the quickest way to get whatever you are holding is to stay away from it until you hand it to him. If he actually looks at you instead of the food, have a party and reinforce that attention! He is figuring out how to ask permission for the things he wants, which reinforces in his mind that you control everything good in his life.

4. Once your dog can ignore a boring treat in your hand for at least ten seconds (without any help from you!), he's ready to be challenged with more difficult distractions. Instead of boring kibble, try a slightly more exciting type of treat. The more valuable the treat is to your dog, the more self-control he will have to muster to leave it alone. Over time, work all the way up to holding his most favorite treat. Be sure to praise him while you are feeding him once he's earned his reward; let him know he's done well when he leaves the treat alone!

Poppy now understands she must exercise self-control even when Dena is holding one of Poppy's favorite treats very close to her nose.

5. When you've worked up to the fantastic treats and your dog is rock solid at least 80% of the time with them, it is time to start introducing really tough challenges into the game. Start practicing with your dog's favorite toy if it can easily be concealed in your hand. Just remember to exhibit self-control yourself and don't move your hand away from your dog if he tries to grab the toy; simply close your hand to conceal the toy until he leaves your hand alone again. You can also introduce a little motion into your training by moving the treat or toy around a little before giving it to him. *Do not tease him with the treat or toy.* Keep the reward at least one foot away from your dog's face and move it slowly side-to-side in

front of him, rather than directly toward his face. Because sporting dogs are hard-wired to be extremely sensitive to motion, it is often hard for them to ignore things that move. If he moves toward the moving object, immediately freeze and hide it in your hand like you did before. When he calms down, move slower and a little further away so he can be successful. If you keep the motion at a distance and don't move the toy directly at your dog, he can learn to have a little more patience when he sees things moving. Be creative with the objects you tempt him with, but don't tease him by shoving the object in his face and then jerking it away. Remember to give him the object as his reward; if he leaves his toy alone, give him the toy as his reward and allow him to play with it!

By gradually building your dog's self-control, you are also indirectly building the amount of time he will stay in one place. If you start asking him to sit and then have him leave an object alone, he is indirectly learning a sit stay. You can also ask him to lie down or stand before asking him to leave something alone to build stays into those positions, too.

Place

Exercise Goal: Your sporting dog will quickly put himself in a safe place between your feet, facing the same direction that you are facing.

Teaching your dog to quickly go between your legs and stand calmly between your feet, facing the same direction that you are, is a very useful behavior for him to learn. If you can teach him this behavior, it will provide you with an easy way to control where your dog is looking. You also subtly assume a more controlling position by standing over your dog, giving him a quiet reminder that no matter how scary or exciting a situation is, you *can*, and will, take care of it. You don't need his help. This has a calming effect on dogs who have been taught to accept this position and have learned to relax there.

1. This is one exercise that is easier to start with your dog off-leash because he will be moving around and between your feet. Start training this in a small, quiet space. This is a perfect exercise to begin in a bathroom because your dog can't wander too far away from you. Have small, tasty treats available in a bowl nearby where you can quickly grab them with either hand.

2. If your dog already knows a hand target, begin your session with a few hand targets. Reach back behind you and ask your dog to come back behind you to touch your hand. If your dog doesn't know how to hand target yet, have him follow a treat in your hand and move him around you. Be sure to move your hand slowly so he can follow the treat and feed him the treat when he catches up to your hand. If he is a master at the Patience is a virtue game, you may need to verbally encourage him to move toward the treat; just be sure that he doesn't grab it out of your hand.

3. Stand with your feet at least shoulder-width apart, facing your dog. With a treat in each hand, lure him around behind you with one hand. With

the other hand, reach between your legs from front to back and either show him a treat to lure him through your legs or present your hand as a hand target and ask him to touch. The closer together you can put your two hands the first few times you do this, the easier it will be for your dog to stop looking at one hand and focus on the other. When you get your dog's attention with the hand between your legs, lure him through between your feet and let him eat his treat while he is still standing between your legs. You and your dog should be facing the same direction at this point. If your dog is too tall to comfortably stand between your legs, lure him into a sit as he comes through your legs. While he is eating his treat, reach in and grab his collar and praise him. Between your feet should always be a safe, fun place to be from your sporting dog's point of view. When he is done eating his treat, you can release him forward and immediately offer him another treat to teach him he still needs to stay focused on you until you tell him he's done, even if he moves out from under you. After he turns to you, feed him another treat, tell him he's free to go, and walk away. Be sure to practice having your dog go around behind from the left side and from the right side so he is comfortable going either way; try to keep his path as close as possible to your body.

Kaija is able to control the direction Tuuri looks by having him go to his "place."

4. When your dog is going around behind you reliably and coming through between your legs at least 80% of the time on both the right and the left, start training in more open areas where he has the chance to move further

from you. If you've thoroughly trained this behavior in a small space such as a bathroom to start with and you are using exciting treats as a lure, he should make the transition with no problems. If he does try to wander away from you when you give him more space, go back to working in a smaller space a little longer. Also, be sure you are moving the treat around your body slow enough that he remains interested in it and will follow it. You can also start narrowing the gap between your feet; ultimately, the gap should be just wide enough for your dog to stand comfortably between your feet with your lower legs lightly touching his sides. Always remember to grab his collar as he is eating his treat and give him praise and pet him to help him relax, too. Keep your knees slightly bent to help you maintain your balance while you are holding your dog.

5. When your dog will come around you quickly and easily, it is time to put the leash on and practice passing the leash between your legs. This is more about training you than the dog, but it is worth the time to work through this. More often than not, your dog will be on-leash when you need to put him in this position, so you both need to know how to work around the leash. Start with your dog on-leash in front of you. Hold the leash in your left hand if you will be asking him to go behind you on the left side or in your right hand if you will be asking him to go around on the right. Signal him to go around you and as he passes behind, drop the leash. When he comes up between your feet, grab the leash as you grab his collar at the same time. Alternatively, as your dog moves to your side, reach between your legs with your free hand and grab ahold of the leash so you don't actually ever let go of it.

6. Once your dog understands where his place is, you can begin to fade the food in your hands and introduce other rewards. A particularly powerful reward for this type of behavior is physical play; when you release your dog, reach back between your legs, put your hands on his rump, and gently push him on through your legs. Most dogs will immediately turn back toward you when you play this silly game, and you can then reward him for giving you attention with some other type of reward. You can also immediately go into a game of Sporting Dog Red Light/Green Light or another training game. The more fun you make this position for your dog, the less stressed he will be if you ever need to put him there to control or protect him.

Having a well-rehearsed safety position can be a lifesaver (literally) for your sporting dog. Of course you must always assess any situation to determine if it is safe and appropriate to confine your dog between your legs; if he is becomes highly aroused and ready to fight, he may redirect his frustration toward you and bite your legs. If another dog is clearly going to attack your dog, it would be safest for you and your dog to drop his leash so he can move without hindrance. But if your dog simply needs to be calmed down or needs a little help staying focused and physically close to you, this is a great behavior to have him perform. With enough practice, you will start to automatically put your dog in his "Place" without even thinking about it when situations become too exciting for him.

Let's put your leash on
Exercise Goal: Your sporting dog will come to you to put his leash on

Dogs tend to react one of two ways toward putting a leash on; either they associate the leash with super fun things like going for a walk and are so excited they can't sit still to have the leash attached, or they associate the leash with all their fun ending and they avoid you any time they see a leash in your hand. Some owners even teach their dogs to go find the leash and bring it to have it attached before going for a walk. Regardless of how your sporting dog responds to the sight of his leash, it is much more pleasant for both of you if you teach your dog to allow you to put on his leash without a fuss. This exercise is an extension of Place, so before starting this exercise, teach your dog to go to his Place.

1. Start training this exercise away from the door that you normally use to leave the house when you and your dog go for a walk. You don't want your dog to get so excited thinking about going for a walk that he can't think about what you are trying to teach him. Have some small, tasty treats handy. Fold up your dog's leash and put it in your back pocket (or in your pant waistband if you don't have pockets). If your dog loses his mind at the sight of his leash, put the leash in your pocket before you get your dog for his training session so he doesn't see it.

2. Practice a few repetitions of Place without the leash on your dog. Remember to grab his collar before you offer him any type of reward, even if you are simply giving him praise for responding to your cue.

3. Have your dog go to Place, grab his collar while praising, take the leash out of your pocket, and quietly clip it on his collar. Drop the leash and reward your dog. Move away from him while encouraging him to come to you with his leash dragging. Have him go to his Place again and remove his leash while rewarding him. If your dog gets goofy and excited by the mere sight of the leash, you are teaching him that putting a leash on leads to rewards for him, but it doesn't always mean you will be going out for a walk. If your dog is stressed by having his leash put on, you are teaching him that the leash leads to many good things. If you do want to go for a walk, move toward the door while he is dragging his leash, have him go to his Place while you stand near the door, pick up his leash, and quickly and calmly go out the door before he gets overly-excited.

Teaching your dog to calmly allow you to put on his leash and readjusting his attitude toward it if he gets either excited or stressed by his leash will make life easier for both of you. This, in turn, starts off your time together on a calmer, more pleasant note. It's a win-win for both of you!

Free ain't free
Exercise Goal: Your sporting dog will remain near you until released, even after his leash is removed.

Many dogs who are well-behaved on-leash simply tune out their owners as soon as their leashes are removed. For them, removing the leash has become a cue that lets them know they are no longer under anyone's direct physical control. Off they charge as soon as the leash comes off, totally disconnected from their owners. Teach your sporting dog to hang around you after you take off his leash and leave only after you give him permission to do so; this will remind him that even without the leash, you are still in charge and everything—including his freedom—comes through you.

This is an exercise that should be worked on every time you take the leash off your dog, including every time you get home from a walk, as well as when you end a formal training session. Consistency is key to successful dog training, so be sure you are consistent in making your dog hang around you after his leash comes off!

1. For this exercise, you will need two leashes. Put a lightweight leash on your dog's collar in addition to his regular leash. Attach both leashes to your dog at the same time so he doesn't realize there's something extra hooked to his collar. Hold both leashes in the same hand as you go for your walk or have a training session.

Robin has two leashes attached to Outlaw's collar—his regular walking leash and a lighter weight one.

2. At the end of your walk or training session, before removing the regular leash from your dog's collar, click the hasp without actually removing the

leash while offering him a small tasty treat. Remain silent while you do this—the sound of the clasp clicking will become a cue to your dog to turn toward you in anticipation of a treat, instead of immediately running off. Repeat this two or three more times without removing the leash, then actually remove the regular leash (leave the lightweight leash on) before you step away. If your sporting dog tries to take off when he feels the weight of the regular leash removed from his neck, the lightweight leash will prevent him from leaving. This will likely surprise him. Step away from him just as if nothing happened and reward him as soon as he reaches you. Put his regular leash back on him while he is eating his treat, walk around a few steps with him, and repeat. When you have finished four or five repetitions, take both leashes off your dog, tell him he is free to go and walk away. His reward for that repetition will be to go do whatever he wants.

Robin offers Outlaw a treat for staying beside her after she removes his regular walking leash. The lighter weight leash prevents him from deciding to leave before Robin tells him he is free to go.

3. Repeat this exercise every time you take the leash off your dog. Before long, you will notice that as soon as he hears the leash clasp click, he will turn toward you. When he is turning toward you at least 80% of the

time, you can eliminate the second leash and start to add in other types of rewards for staying near you after his leash is removed. Most of the time his reward will simply be praise and being released to do whatever he wants. But now he is waiting for you to tell him to leave you, instead of taking off on his own. Every once in a while, give him a treat, let him outside, or grab a toy and start playing with him after you remove the leash. Keep him guessing when and if you will give him a special reward and he will be more willing to hang around with you after you take the leash off, just to see what's going to happen.

Teaching your dog to stay near you after you take his leash off is a good safety behavior for him to learn. If his collar slips off or his leash breaks, you have a reasonable chance of getting ahold of him if he knows it is worth his while to stay with you. This is an easy behavior to teach; just be sure you work on it every time you take his leash off, even if you aren't having a formal training session with him.

Oh @%*#!!

Exercise Goal: Your sporting dog will come toward you, even if your voice sounds stressed.

Sporting dogs were bred to work closely with humans. They tend to bond strongly to their families and are quite sensitive to changes in body language, voice, and behavior. They are also a curious bunch of busy bodies by nature and, if given the chance, many would be more than happy to head off down the road in search of adventure (or birds), particularly if they are never given the chance to explore with you. Some try to make this dream come true by waltzing out the front door, trotting off through the back gate, or tunneling under or scaling over the fence. If you are lucky, you will see this escape attempt and can thwart it before your dog gets very far down the road. But sometimes, in your haste to keep your dog from heading off into the sunset, you yell in an attempt to stop him and end up scaring him away rather than encouraging him back to you. Getting your dog used to obeying you even when your voice is strained and/or loud greatly increases the chances of getting your dog to respond to you, regardless of the situation. Remember that dogs are fantastic discriminators, and they will respond (or not respond) to changes in the tone and volume of your voice. Playing the Oh @%*# (substitute the four-letter word of your choice here) game is an easy way to work on this.

1. Start this exercise with your dog on-leash in a quiet, calm environment. Have small, tasty treats available for rewards. Keep the treats in your pocket or in a bowl nearby so your dog won't be distracted by them. Sit or step on the end of the leash so your dog can't decide to walk away while you are training. If you have young, impressionable children, keep them out of the room so they don't learn any new words you might not want repeated in public!

2. Think of a phrase or two you are apt to spontaneously say if, as you open the door, you see your dog zip past you toward the wide open spaces of the neighborhood. Be honest here—the kids should be in another room and if your inclination would be to say something a little off-color, so

be it. It is best to play this game using the actual words that are likely to come out of your mouth in a moment of panic or stress so your dog gets used to them.

3. Say your stress phrase of choice in a normal speaking voice, followed immediately by a tasty treat. Your dog doesn't have to do anything when you make your statement. You are starting to build this statement into a cue that you will give your dog something good whenever you say this. Repeat your phrase in a normal speaking voice four more times, rewarding after each repetition.

4. If your dog doesn't flinch or act afraid of this tone of voice, increase the volume slightly the next training session. Your dog shouldn't be afraid of your voice. Try not to be "corrective" with your voice as you increase the volume. Keep your voice sounding normal, just make it louder. If you use a low, growly voice as you increase your volume, your dog may think you are scolding him. This will likely confuse your dog and decrease the chances he will want to come to you. If you gradually change the tone and volume of your voice, your dog will soon learn to not be concerned by such changes.

5. Once your dog is used to your voice being loud, start adding in as much stress as you can. Imagine your dog darting out your front door, heading for the street, just as a car comes around the corner toward your house. Imagine the fear you would feel thinking your dog will be hit by a car and killed, right in front of you and your family. Try to project that fear in your voice as you practice this game; your dog should notice the difference in your body language and voice. This is what your dog would actually experience if he ever does get out into an unfenced area, so practice this in the safety of your home to help your dog remain calm, even when you aren't. Fear often makes a person's voice rise in pitch. Be sure you aren't using a corrective tone as you practice this version of your phrase.

6. Practice this game with many different phrases, including the dog's name and common commands that your dog knows very well (for example, "Come" and "Sit"). Be sure your dog doesn't perceive the change in your voice as a correction. Pay attention to your dog's behavior and body language, and if you ask him to perform a behavior, don't forget to help him perform the correct behavior if he gets confused by the tone of your voice. If your dog seems scared or confused, make your words quieter and gradually build back up to a louder level.

By playing this game, you increase the odds that if you ever yell out in panic at your dog, he will turn toward you in happy anticipation of a reward rather than continue trucking on down the street away from you in fear.

Poppy is curious, but definitely not afraid, when her owners talk to her in loud, excited voices.

Doorbell ding dongs

Exercise Goal: Your sporting dog will remain calm when guests enter your home.

Many dogs start barking when they hear the doorbell ring. We tend to reinforce this type of behavior by the way we greet our dogs every time we come home. Our dogs are generally glad to see us, and we are glad to see them. So what do we do? We talk goofy, pet them, let them jump up on us, and, in general, encourage them to be pretty darn naughty while they are greeting us. Dog-loving guests and children that come to our homes usually do the same thing. So we create little ding dongs out of our dogs by the way we greet them every day, but then wonder why it is so hard to keep those same dogs from barking every time the doorbell rings or jumping up on Great Aunt Edna when she comes through the door. To teach your dog to be quieter when the doorbell rings and calmer when guests come over, you will need to manage his behavior by greeting him more calmly yourself and by not allowing your dog near the door when guests arrive, unless he is on leash and supervised. When you are gone during the day, you can crate your dog or confine him to another part of the house away from the door so he can't rush you as you walk in the house. Combine this with teaching him that the sound of the doorbell or the door lock means that good things are coming from somewhere other than the person coming through the door and you will be able to gain control of the situation and teach your sporting dog to behave more appropriately at the door. Of course, you will also need to teach your family and guests how to behave more appropriately as well by sharing with them how to behave to help you with your dog's training. Chances are they will be so appreciative of your efforts, they will gladly help out!

1. You will need to find a place outside near your door to store a tightly-closed container of treats before you start this exercise. You need to be able to reach the container and get some treats out before you open the door. You will also need to get treats before you let guests in your home, so you will need to find a place to store a second container inside the house near the door. Be sure the place you store your treats is inaccessible to your dog and not in direct sunlight where the treats may become rancid over time. Only put enough treats in the containers to last a few days to keep them fresh and safe to feed your dog.

2. Start this training when you aren't actually coming home from being gone all day. Pick up your keys and anything else you regularly take with you when you leave the house (purse, briefcase, etc.) and go out the door you usually leave through when you go away to work or to run errands. If you drive away each morning, get in your car and drive around the block. Come back, park your car in its usual spot, and go up to the door you normally come through when you get back home. Everything you do should be exactly what you do when you leave your house for an extended period of time. The only difference is that you are only gone for a few minutes. Keeping your absence brief at first will keep your dog a little calmer when you come back in.

3. Before opening the door and stepping inside, grab several treats out of the treat container you have near the door. Put your key in the doorknob and open the door. As soon as you step inside the house and your dog starts to approach you, toss the treats out a few feet in front of you. Remain silent and ignore your dog; you want him to chase after his treats. Because you haven't been gone that long, he shouldn't be so excited to see you that you can't get him to go after his treats. If he meets you at the door when you come in, ignore him and toss the treats anyway. By tossing treats away from you, he will start to associate the sound of the door opening with eating and he will start to move away from you in anticipation of getting his treats.

4. After he eats his treats, if he comes up to you, calmly and quietly give him a few pats while he has all four feet on the floor. If he jumps on you, ignore him and go about your business. Literally turn your back on the dog and walk away. Avoid making any eye contact, physical contact (like pushing him off you), or talking to him if he jumps up on you. All of these things, from your dog's point of view, are rewarding, because you are giving him the attention he is trying to get by jumping up on you in the first place. Deprive him of all attention and even your presence if he jumps up on you and give him quiet, calm praise and petting when he remains on the floor for your attention to help him understand what behavior is expected from him. It may take some time for him to

start controlling himself when you come inside. The longer he has been allowed to go crazy at the door, the longer it will take to retrain him to behave more appropriately. Repeat this process every time family members come home and he will start to associate someone coming through the door with moving away for a treat, and being calm with getting attention. If you are concerned about giving your dog too many treats while you are training this behavior, take a small portion of his kibble and set it aside to use as training treats so you don't increase his total daily caloric intake. If your dog is more motivated by toys than treats, you can substitute a toy for this training.

5. A knock on the door or the sound of the doorbell usually precedes guests coming inside your home. These sounds will cause many dogs to bark and get excited before they even see the person waiting at the door. If you know you will have company arriving and want to work on teaching your dog to remain calm when he hears the doorbell, put a leash on your dog and tether him to you before you expect your guest to arrive. Have small, tasty treats handy. When the doorbell rings, calmly drop a treat on the ground near you and as soon as your dog takes the treat, take another step toward the door, drop a treat and repeat until you reach the door. If you are using treats that are extra special for your dog, he will quickly figure out that looking around for treats when he hears the doorbell pays off for him; barking at the sound doesn't. When you reach the door, keep the leash short and toss a few treats behind you as you let your guest inside. It is important that your guest not talk or look at your dog as he comes inside; if your dog remains calm, your guest can quietly greet your dog briefly after he has come inside and the door is closed. If the person is too young or too unreliable to ignore your dog or your dog is just too excited to physically control, you may want to treat the dog when the doorbell rings as above, but instead of walking toward the door, walk toward your dog's crate or into another room where he can wait until your guest has come inside. Leave several treats in the area you leave your dog in and walk away quietly. When your dog calms down, you can put him on a leash and allow him to say hello to your guest, as long as he keeps all four feet on the floor. If your dog barks after you leave, ignore him until he quiets down. Then put a leash on him and bring him out to greet your guest.

6. If you are one of the lucky few who own a sporting dog that doesn't bark at the doorbell, you can simply put a leash on your dog and grab a few treats before you open the door to train him to be calm around company. Review Step 5 above to help him learn to remain calm when people come in your house.

7. Once you notice your dog starting to sniff around for his treats as soon as he hears the doorbell ring, start to fade away the treats and replace them with allowing your dog to greet your guest at the door (as long as he remains calm and on the floor and you put a leash on him before you open the door). If he starts jumping or barking as your guest enters, toss a few treats on the floor to redirect his attention away from the person

and back away so he doesn't have the chance to jump up or get even more excited. Be sure to remain calm yourself, even though your dog didn't respond as you wanted him to. Go back to Step 5 for a few more sessions before trying to fade the treats away again. This exercise takes patience, but it is well worth it! Eventually, you will be able to allow your dog to greet people without putting his leash on, but that will take time. It is easier to put a leash on and not waste a training opportunity than to risk your dog reverting to his old behaviors when he doesn't have a leash on and there is nothing you can really do to stop him.

Teaching your dog to remain calm when people come into your home is an effort that both you and your house guests will appreciate. The calmer your dog remains when he hears the doorbell, the less likely he will be to rush the door, jump up on guests, and possibly end up outside. And if he does manage to get outside, a calm sporting dog is far easier to get back inside than an excited one.

> Dear Family, Friends, and Delivery People,
>
> Please give us a few extra moments to answer the door. As a favor to our guests, we are teaching Triever to be polite when people enter our home. It will take a little more time for us to let you in because we need to put Triever on a leash before we open the door.
>
> To help us with his training, please ignore Triever when you come inside. He can only be petted after he calms down and behaves appropriately.
>
> Thanks for your patience! Triever and his Family

If you are concerned guests will become impatient waiting for you to put your dog on a leash, make a fun sign to put on your front door while you are teaching your dog how to greet guests politely to let people know that it may take you a little longer to come to the door.

Conclusion

Taking the time to learn good management techniques and teach your sporting dog how to cope better with exciting things in his environment will go a long way toward reducing the problematic behaviors most of us deal with at some point in a sporting dog's life. The excessive *joie de vivre* and close bonding to people in our modern sporting dogs can make life with one difficult at times. But these same attributes also give our dogs their unique, loveable, family-oriented outlook on life that enticed many of us to bring a sporting dog into our homes in the first place. Sporting dogs need to be sporting dogs sometimes to be physically and mentally healthy. And no amount of training will remove sporting dog traits from these dogs. But by working with these traits and modifying them through careful training, you can help your dog cope better with the distractions of urban life, without completely extinguishing that joyful sporting dog personality.

Chapter 10

Management and Training for

Distractibility

...he advances...his wet nose screening a hundred scents for that one scent... which gives life and meaning to the whole landscape. Partridge scent is the gold standard that relates his world to mine.

~ Aldo Leopold
American ecologist

Most sporting dogs are naturally sensitive to motion and smells as a result of their strong hunting instincts. Generations of sporting dogs were selectively bred to locate downed prey quickly and effectively, giving us the dogs we own today. There are several management techniques and training exercises you can use to help your sporting dog overcome his natural tendency to get distracted by sights and smells, while at the same time building his trust and confidence in you.

Management techniques

Divide and conquer

Have you ever tried to hold a phone conversation while a young child constantly tugs on your clothes, asking you something over and over and over and over and over and over again? If so, you know that such a distraction makes it difficult to stay completely focused on your conversation. Even though most of us can tune out verbal nagging fairly well, it is nearly impossible to completely block out repetitive physical contact. You may still be able to do the task you are working on, but you usually find yourself remaining consciously aware of the physical contact, and undoubtedly a little distracted by it.

It is the same for your dog. Repetitive physical contact is harder for him to ignore than repetitive verbal cues. Touching your dog repetitively when he is intently focused on something else is a good management technique to use when you need to pull out all the stops to get your dog refocused on you. When you do this, at least a small bit of his attention will be focused on your touches instead of whatever he is staring at or sniffing. This is not the rewarding type of contact you would use if you liked the behavior your dog is doing, but rather, it should be a slightly irritating type of contact, like a child tugging on your sleeve. Tickling the dog's ear, playfully tweaking his tail, or some other non-painful contact that your dog isn't afraid of but, at the same time, doesn't overly enjoy, can help divert some of his attention away from whatever has caught his eye and direct it back to you. When you get his attention, even for only a micro-moment, you can then give him a cue for a more acceptable behavior to do or add in other management techniques to help him behave more appropriately for you.

Belle can't stay completely focused on the photographer when Bethany tickles her head in an annoying way.

Thirty second sight and sniff fest

If you've ever tried to lose weight, you know that cravings are the undoing of many dieters. Often a dieter will experience certain food cravings if he is limiting his food choices; usually, the more restrictive the diet, the more intense the cravings. Some people can resist cravings until the desire passes, but most dieters become fixated on the craving and can think of little else until they finally give in and eat whatever food it is that they are longing for. If they eat just a tiny bit of that special food, the craving will start to subside and little, if any, harm is done to the dieting efforts in the long run. But if they keep trying to deny themselves that food completely, they may very well end up totally absorbed with the desire to get that food and when they finally get it, they overeat and derail their weight loss efforts.

Sporting dogs can develop cravings, too. These dogs can quickly become fixated on sights and smells as a result of their hunting heritages. If you continually deny your dog the opportunity to check out his environment visually, or to investigate intriguing scents, you won't be decreasing his interest in these things; you will be creating instinctual cravings that can eventually become so strong your dog will completely lose focus on you and "gorge" himself on watching everything going on around him and sniffing every single blade of grass he can get to. By allowing your dog about thirty seconds to investigate his environment with his nose and eyes, you can start to diminish those cravings, just like the dieter who is craving chocolate and eats one small square of dark chocolate every day to make the craving subside. This dieter becomes more likely to lose weight in the long run than the dieter who tries to deny himself any chocolate whatsoever until one day, he snaps and eats an entire 5 lb. milk chocolate bar in one afternoon. If your dog is routinely provided an opportunity to investigate his environment, he won't be as apt to frantically try to steal the chance to satisfy his instinctual cravings and quit paying attention to you. Simply allow your dog to do as he pleases (as long as he isn't pulling you all over the place to investigate) for thirty seconds, then firmly and calmly ask for a simple behavior he knows. If he performs the behavior, you can either reward his compliance by allowing him to go back to his investigations, or you can reward him in some other manner and continue to ask him to work with you. If he doesn't perform the behavior, help him do it, then move him away from the area he was investigating until he is far enough away he can listen to you again.

Because Dezi is regularly allowed to explore her environment, she is able to better ignore distractions when her owner asks her to pay attention.

Training exercises

Heavenly head holds

Exercise Goal: Your sporting dog will allow you to gently hold his head and redirect his attention.

When dogs are in a training class and all of a sudden one starts barking, seemingly out of the clear blue, it usually happens because either the barking dog is just overly excited in general, or because another dog is quietly sitting there making inappropriate eye contact with him and he finally lost his patience with such rude canine behavior. Either way, being able to do head holds with your dog is a handy way to help keep your sporting dog relaxed and more focused on you than on distractions in these types of situations. This game is useful as a management technique to help your dog calm down and will also help you both enjoy a few moments of focused attention with each other, but may require some actual training to get your dog comfortable with you holding his head. This is *not a scruff shake, alpha roll or any other type of physical correction;* this technique simply involves cradling your dog's head in your hands and gently redirecting his attention toward you. Most dogs resist having their head controlled at first, so be patient and persistent. Your dog can learn to enjoy having his head gently held and controlled.

One important thing to remember with this game is that sporting dogs instinctually become very focused on things that move in their environment. Once he gets distracted by something, it will be very hard for him to turn his back on whatever grabbed his attention. The key to this game is to use it as a tool to *prevent* your dog from becoming distracted or overly excited in the first place, rather than as a way to calm him down after he has crossed over into "crazy land."

1. Start this exercise in a quiet, calm environment where you can sit comfortably. Your dog must be wearing a buckle collar for this game, even if he also has a harness on, and the collar must be loose enough for you to slide your fingers between it and your dog's neck. Your dog should be on-leash. To make it easier for both of you, work on this exercise when your dog is already fairly calm. Step or sit on the end of the leash so your dog can't decide to walk away while you are training, leaving both your hands free to cradle your dog's head. Be sure there is enough slack in the leash for your dog to sit or stand. The reward for this exercise will be your calm praise and gentle touch.

2. Sit on a chair facing your dog. It doesn't matter what position your dog is in, but this game is easier to teach if you are sitting comfortably. Adjust your dog's collar so it is resting high up on his neck, just behind his ears. Gently reach under his chin with both hands, palms facing up. Stick your fingertips up under your dog's collar, palms still facing up. If you have a big dog, slide your hands apart slightly so you can rest the corners of your dog's lower jaw, just below his ears, in your palms, keeping your fingertips under the collar to prevent your dog from pulling away from you. Place your thumbs on each side of your dog's head just below his ears. Your dog's head should now be resting on your palms and your thumbs are resting on both sides of his head. In this position, you can gently control how much your dog can move his head simply by bracing your hands against his motion.

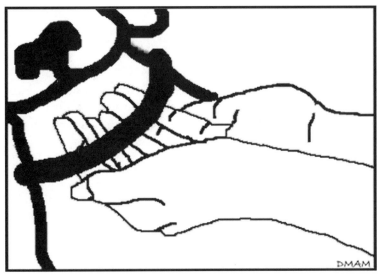

Be sure to slide your fingertips underneath your dog's collar before you try to cradle his head so he can't pull away from you.

3. Talk calmly and quietly to your dog. Don't stare at him—this isn't an attention exercise, but rather a relaxation exercise. If he is calm with this position, praise and release him. If he actively tries to throw your hands off his head, continue to calmly and gently hold his head until he briefly stops moving. Don't scold him or yank on him; just hold on to him and go with his movements until he calms down. When he stops moving, praise and release him. Remember that it is against his nature to allow his view of his environment to be restricted, so he has to learn that when you hold him like this, he can relax and trust you that there isn't anything around that he needs to look at.

4. Very gradually increase the amount of time you hold your dog's head as he becomes more comfortable with your restraint. Over time, you will find that you don't need to put your fingertips under his collar; you can just put your hands under his chin. When you no longer need to hold the collar to control his head, start adding in gentle massage touches along his muzzle and ears, using your thumbs. Your ultimate goal is to have your dog physically relax in this position. A nice additional benefit of this exercise is that as you focus on relaxing your dog, you will also relax!

Once your dog begins to enjoy having his head held, you can use this proactively in potentially exciting situations to keep him calm. This is a great exercise to do while you are waiting for your training class to start; once you find your seat, start relaxing your dog. You will be surprised how much more you will be able to accomplish in class if your dog starts his lessons relaxed and happy!

You talkin' to me?

Exercise Goal: Your sporting dog will look toward you when you say his name.

How many times a day do you say your dog's name? How many times do you pair his name with some type of correction? "Triever, no!" "Triever, get off that!" "Bad dog, Triever!" Eventually, your dog learns to tune out his name or, worse yet, links his name with an imminent correction from you. If your dog associates his name with positive things, you will always have a handy way to quickly gain his attention when you need it, simply by saying his name.

1. This exercise can be practiced anywhere, any time. You can use any type of reward with this exercise. Provide a different type of reward each training session to keep your sporting dog guessing what fun will follow his name. Be careful that you don't show the reward to your dog before you say his name; you don't want to bribe him to look at you.

2. Start this exercise with your dog on leash so he can't walk away from you. Say your dog's name once in a pleasant tone, followed immediately by a reward. Repeat five times per session and try to do several sessions each day. It doesn't matter if he looks at you when you say his name for the first few sessions; reward him anyway so you can rebuild the positive association he has with his name. With enough repetitions, he will begin to associate his name with getting a reward and will start to look at you when you say his name.

3. As your training progresses, you will notice your dog will start to turn toward you as soon as he hears his name. When he is looking at you immediately after hearing his name at least 80% of the time (four out five repetitions), you can begin to pair his name with another cue he knows, such as "Sit" or "Down." Immediately follow the second cue with a reward. Keep the behavior you want quick and easy to perform. Grabbing your dog's attention by saying his name before you give him a cue will help him focus on the behavior he should perform.

4. Once your dog has relearned the value of his name, you can also use it as a fun way to build an emergency backup recall for your dog. Take him out for a walk on a long line or a thin rope with a clasp tied to the end so he can move away from you, without being able to actually run away from you. Let him get distracted enough to look away from you, then call his name once and start moving toward something, as if you are hunting. Run to a tree and look up in the branches, dig around in a patch of weeds, or look under a rock. Act like whatever you are looking at is the most interesting thing that ever existed and ignore your dog (since he's on his leash, you know he can't run away). When your dog hears his name and turns toward you, he'll see you engaging in an interesting hunt. If you are doing a good job of enjoying your special "hunt," he will probably come to you even though you didn't ask him to come. Praise him profusely and reward him by allowing him to thoroughly check out the place you were looking for a bit before continuing your walk. Every once in awhile make things extra exciting by dropping his favorite toy or

a small treat where you were hunting so he can find it when he comes over to investigate. This is *not* a replacement for training your dog to come on cue; it is a supplemental way to encourage your dog to move toward you using his name only. You still need to teach your dog to come with a recall cue as well.

Your dog should always associate his name with pleasant interactions with you. Think like a sporting dog and strengthen that association by hunting together. You are teaching your dog that paying attention to you and being around you is fun, even when you are outdoors, and that his name means something good is coming from you.

The eyes have it

Exercise Goal: Your sporting dog will give you direct eye contact on cue.

Controlling your sporting dog's eyes will go a long way toward controlling his behavior. If your dog is looking at you, he can't also be looking at the dog walking across the street, the bird in the tree, or the toy in the yard. But it is important to remember that in canine language, staring can be very intimidating and confrontational. Your dog may feel uncomfortable staring at you because in his native language, staring is rude. Be sure you keep a pleasant expression on your face and don't loom over your dog while you teach him this behavior so he will feel comfortable looking you in the eye. Make sure you blink and breathe normally, too!

1. If you've worked on all the other training exercises up to this point, you already know the first step—start this exercise with your dog on-leash in a quiet, calm environment. Have small, tasty treats available for rewards. Keep the treats in your pocket or in a bowl nearby so your dog won't be distracted by them. Sit or step on the end of the leash so your dog can't decide to walk away while you are training.

2. Take one treat, show it to your dog, move it up to your face and hold it between your eyes. Don't say anything to your dog; let the treat do all the talking for you in this step. If the treat is one your dog really likes, he will naturally follow the treat up to your face and make eye contact with you. The moment his eyes meet yours, praise and give him the treat. Yes, in this step, the attention is really all about the treat. But using a treat is a quick and easy way to teach your dog that it is OK to look you straight in the eyes. That is all you are trying to teach him at this point.

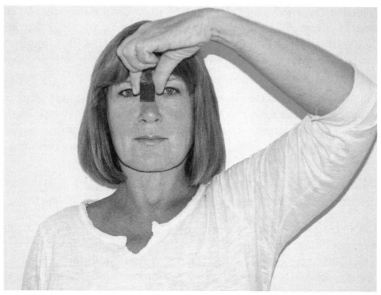

Let the treat guide your dog's eyes into yours. Eventually you will not need the treat on your face to get eye contact from your dog.

3. To help your dog understand he can look at your eyes from any position he is in, practice having him watch you while he is in different positions (sit, down, stand) and while he is in different positions relative to you (in front of you, beside you, at various angles to you). If you only train eye contact when your dog is sitting straight in front of you, he won't necessarily understand what you want when you ask him to give you eye contact when he is walking beside you or lying near you.

4. Once your dog will immediately follow the treat up to your face and give you eye contact at least 80% of the time in a quiet environment, begin adding some slightly more difficult distractions to your training session. Don't worry about increasing the length of time your dog is watching you or moving the treat away from your eyes just yet. The first step in developing fluency will focus on ignoring environmental distractions for very short periods of time. Using the distraction list you created in Chapter 7 as your training guide, work up to at least 80% reliability on moderately difficult distractions for your dog before moving to the next step.

5. When your dog understands how to make eye contact with you for short periods of time in fairly distracting environments, start getting rid of the treat stuck between your eyes. Start this step in an environment with few distractions. Bring your hand up between your eyes as you've been doing, then across your face and stop with your hand next to your ear. Your sporting dog will probably follow your hand as it moves; remain silent and wait for him to look back in your eyes. It may take a few moments, but he will eventually look back at you. The split second he makes eye contact, praise and give him the treat. With a few repetitions, he will figure out that looking in your eyes, rather than at your hand, earns him

the treat. Once he will quickly look at your eyes at least 80% of the time when you move your hand away from your eyes, add back in the position and distraction work as you did in Steps 3 and 4.

6. You can now pair a verbal cue with your hand cue. Simply say your watch cue as you bring your hand up to your face. Because you have worked for several sessions to get your dog fluent with the behavior, you can be fairly certain he will actually watch you even though he hasn't yet learned what your verbal cue means; he only knows what your hand motion means. By pairing the verbal cue with the hand cue, over time your dog will associate the verbal cue with the behavior.

7. Continue to fade the use of treats by moving your treat hand up to your eyes, across to your ear, then let your wrist go limp and your hand drop to your shoulder. As before, if your dog follows your hand, resist the urge to say anything or repeat your verbal cue. Simply wait for him to look back in your eyes, then praise and treat.

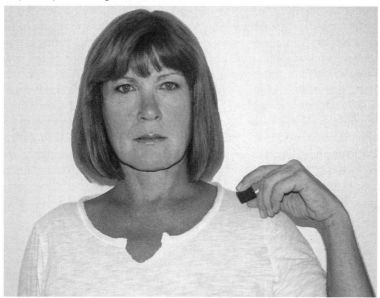

Have patience while your dog figures out he will get the treat if he looks at your eyes, instead of your hand.

8. The last step in getting rid of the treat is to move your hand up to your eyes, across to your ear, down to your shoulder, then drop your arm to your side. Wait silently if your dog follows your hand with his eyes. This is a particularly difficult step for most dogs because now your hand is at or very near their eye level, making it harder to ignore. Be patient and quiet while he figures out he still needs to look at your eyes to earn his treat. Once you have 80% reliability with your hand at your side, you can eliminate the treat in your hand altogether. You will still move your hand in the same way as if you had a treat, but the treat will remain hidden somewhere else until he has given you attention. You should always

reward his attention, but you can begin to use other types of rewards (praise, pats, going outside) in place of treats when he looks at you.

9. One of the last attention skills to add is duration. This is accomplished by simply delaying the delivery of the reward after your dog gives you eye contact. Instead of immediately giving him his treat after he gives you eye contact, you will start to wait short periods of time before rewarding him. Be sure to increase the amount of time he must look at you to earn his reward in small increments so he can be successful. Increasing the duration in one or two second intervals will help you progress slowly but steadily toward your ultimate duration goal.

10. Keep in mind that dogs are masters at identifying environmental patterns. As you work on increasing duration, remember that if you always give him his treat after he gives you fixed number of seconds of eye contact, he may begin to quit looking at you after that amount of time in anticipation of receiving his reward, whether or not you were ready to actually give it to him. A good way to keep him from predicting exactly how long he has to look at you to earn his reward is to vary how long you have him give you eye contact on every repetition you complete during a training session. For example, if you are working for ten seconds of eye contact, start by doing a repetition that is two seconds long, then five seconds long, then one second long, then eight seconds long, then three seconds long, then ten seconds long, then two seconds long, and end with eleven seconds. Your dog won't be able to predict when you are going to release and reward him. He will get some easier repetitions mixed in with more difficult ones. There is no special formula for setting the pattern of your repetitions; just mix up two or three shorter than your target duration, two or three at your target duration, and at least one slightly longer than your current target duration during your training session to help minimize anticipation problems and increase duration.

Before starting to teach Maya moving eye contact, Linda has helped Maya become fluent in stationary eye contact around various distractions, including Maya's favorite toy.

11. There will be times you want or need your dog to give you attention for short periods of time while you are walking (e.g., when you are passing a distraction). You can teach him how to do this once he is fluent in giving you eye contact without moving. When you add motion to attention work, start with your dog standing beside you. It is easier for your dog to maintain eye contact when he is already standing; when a dog gets up from a sit, his head is naturally inclined to drop, so it is more difficult for him to keep watching you if he has to get up from a sit to start walking with you. Go back to holding a treat near your eyes for the first few sessions to help him understand what you want while you are moving. You may need to twist slightly toward your dog so he can see your eyes and the treat in your hand until he figures out he can give you eye contact and walk at the same time, but as soon as he is giving you a few steps of moving eye contact, straighten your body back into your natural walking position so he can learn how to see your face when you are standing

facing straight forward. Cue him with your hand and voice to look at you, and once you have eye contact, take one or two steps forward, and praise and reward him if he is still giving you eye contact. If he isn't, quietly try again. If your dog can't do two steps without breaking eye contact, try a single step. If he can't do that, go back and work on the stationary attention a few more sessions to be sure he really understands the basic concept of watching you. As your dog becomes more comfortable watching you while you move, you can gradually add in more steps the same way you increased time in Step 10, and later, increase the difficulty of the distractions he must ignore while giving you moving eye contact.

Karen cues Keagan to give her eye contact by pointing at her eyes as they are walking.

Teaching your sporting dog to give you eye contact around distractions takes time, but once he understands how to pay attention to you on cue, you will be able to make more progress controlling other aspects of his behavior. Remember that you must watch your dog when your dog watches you, so it isn't realistic to expect strict attention from your dog for the entire duration of a walk. But it is realistic to ask for a few steps of focused attention at random times during your walk; you can then allow your dog to look around and enjoy his walk as his reward for staying focused on you for short distances.

Hello, Sunshine!

Exercise Goal: Your sporting dog will voluntarily check in with you

Rewarding active attention is another way to encourage your sporting dog to pay more attention to you. The reason this is called "active" attention is because your *dog* is actively choosing to look at you. You aren't doing anything to encourage his attention like we did in The Eyes Have It exercise. This is the type of attention your dog voluntarily offers when he looks up at you as you walk by, or when he actually seeks you out to be near you. This is *not* the kind of attention you get from him when you are sitting on the couch eating a bowl of hot, buttery popcorn or when you are holding a dog treat in your hand—that type of attention is all about the food, not you. Active attention is the type of attention your sporting dog gives you simply because you are both in the same space at the same time and he recognizes you as someone worth paying attention to in his life. Because dogs are social animals, they naturally pay attention to other members of their pack. You can take advantage of that instinct to encourage you dog to voluntarily pay more attention to you.

This is an easy exercise to do, but it does require you to start paying a little more attention to your dog. The next time you walk through a room where your dog is and he looks up at you, just say something pleasant to him, like "Hello, Sunshine! What a good dog!" as you pass by. Don't make a big fuss or give him a treat. Simply acknowledge with a few words of sincere praise that you see him looking at you, to let him know that paying attention to you is a really great thing for him to do. Then continue on about your business. He doesn't have to get up and come to you or stare at you for any length of time. In fact, you don't want to encourage any type of behavior other than him checking in with you as you pass by. If he chooses to come to you, continue to do whatever you are doing and give him a few more words of quiet praise, but don't make a big deal over him. You don't want him to think you expect him to follow you around constantly. You are simply encouraging him to check in with you when you are around.

By acknowledging the times when your sporting dog looks at you of his own free will, you will also be developing a good training habit in yourself. You will start to recognize the good behaviors your dog does, instead of only the less desirable ones. It is very easy to fall into the training trap of focusing solely on the behaviors you want to change in your dog and losing sight of all the good behaviors your dog already does. This shift in perspective will help you enjoy your dog more and give you more patience to teach him how you expect him to behave.

Chapter 11

Management and Training for an "Oral" Lifestyle

A dog in his kennel barks at his fleas; a dog hunting doesn't notice them.

~ Chinese proverb

The oral habits of sporting dogs drive most owners crazy if they don't know how to properly channel those instinctive behaviors in an appropriate direction. Whether he is happy, sad, eager, anxious, or frustrated, the average sporting dog looks for something to hold in his mouth when his emotions are running high. Holding something in his mouth can have a calming effect on the dog. First-time sporting dog owners can be caught off guard by the amount of destruction an untrained, under-exercised, unmanaged sporting dog can do with his mouth in a relatively short period of time. By teaching your puppy good "mouth manners" from the start, you can avoid much of that frustration with your dog.

Management techniques

Quid pro quo

A common complaint from many sporting dog owners is their dogs are always grabbing things around the house and running off with them—dog toys, kid toys, shoes, small pieces of furniture—pretty much anything that fits in the mouth is fair game to be carried around and, quite possibly, chewed up. This annoying habit is particularly prevalent in puppies and adolescent dogs who are teething. Chewing is a natural stress reliever, as well as a way to help baby teeth fall out and adult teeth come in. Dogs enjoy games of chase, and many times that is what follows when a dog grabs a forbidden item; his owner immediately starts chasing him around in an attempt to get the item away from him. From the dog's point of view, picking up things and running off with them to start a game of chase is fun! Combine that with a strong instinct to retrieve, and it is little wonder that many sporting dog owners get frustrated with their dogs' oral lifestyle.

While the obvious solution to this problem is to keep everything you don't want ending up in your dog's mouth well out of your dog's reach, this isn't practical in most homes. Clothing and shoes end up on the floor or in accessible laundry baskets, human toys aren't always picked up, and items like bath soap and toilet paper are ordinarily kept in places that are dog-accessible. Minimizing the ancillary fun your dog has when he is holding something inappropriate in his mouth is important. If you chase, yell, grab at, or otherwise engage your dog in any activity remotely resembling "play" to him, you are actually teaching him that the way to get attention and play from you is to put something in his mouth! If you move too quickly toward him, you might also cause him to try to swallow whatever he is holding, which can have very serious health consequences. Be sure to contact your veterinarian immediately if your dog swallows anything that isn't meant to be eaten or if he swallows any large cooked bones or other solid food items that could possibly cause an intestinal blockage. It is always better to be overly-cautious and spend a few dollars to have your veterinarian induce vomiting so your dog is safe, than to assume your dog will be able to pass what he swallowed and later learn he has an intestinal blockage that will be fatal without timely, successful, expensive, veterinary intervention.

By calmly offering your dog something else in exchange for what he has in his mouth, you can teach your dog to bring things *to* you as bartering chips to get other things *from* you that he also wants. The key here is that the item you have is something that, at the very least, is equally desirable to your dog as what he has in his mouth at the moment. Most of the time the item your dog is holding is not all that interesting to him on its own; the item is merely his way to engage you in play. If you take the time to make a reward list like we explored in Chapter 6 and rank those rewards in terms of how desirable they are to your dog, you should be able to come up with something that you can offer your dog that will trump whatever he is holding in his mouth. Even if you don't have a really desirable treat in your hand or his favorite toy in your pocket at the moment your dog picks up something he shouldn't have, you can still use this technique; encourage him to follow you as you excitedly move toward the treat jar or refrigerator (a small piece of human food works wonders in these situations) or toward wherever his favorite toy is. By distracting him in this manner, he will either carry the forbidden item with him as he follows you, or he might spit it out. If he spits it out, pick it up, but be sure to follow through with a reward anyway!

Of course, this assumes that he isn't running around with a dead, stinky animal or something similarly crazy-good to him. Those situations will likely require you to calmly and quietly try to walk him into a corner where you can then get ahold of him and gently take the item out of his mouth. If you chase him or move too fast, you may encourage him to gulp the item down and the result a few minutes or a few hours later is apt to be even more disgusting than the original item. Most sporting dogs are highly food motivated. A tasty treat is often all that is necessary to get your dog to drop what he has and come to you. You must maintain a calm, welcoming demeanor while offering your dog his alternative reward. Stand still and ask your dog to come to you or walk away and encourage him to follow. Even if he doesn't drop the item he is holding, if he comes to you and you move slowly and deliberately, you should be able to gently grab his collar, take the item from his mouth, and give him his treat. You are rewarding him for coming to you, even though you may have to take the item out of his mouth. Always reward your dog for coming to you, no matter how frustrated you are with him. If you look angry, talk harshly, and move quickly, you will discourage him from wanting to be anywhere within arm's reach of you. If he drops the item and then comes to you, praise him for dropping the item and encourage him to come to you and offer him his reward. Be sure your dog comes to you, instead of you going to your dog, if at all possible. If you want, pick a cue and repeat it while you are making your item exchange with your dog. For example, as your dog approaches, you might pleasantly ask him "Can I have that?" while he is holding the item you want to get away from him. With repetition, he will associate that question with spitting out whatever he is holding to get something even better from you. And if you don't get in enough repetitions for your dog to learn that on cue, good for you! That means your dog isn't picking up forbidden items very often, which is what you want in the first place.

Bonkers for binkies

Nearly all sporting dog breeds I have included in this book can be used to retrieve downed game, and as a result, these dogs tend to be very oral. Sometimes simply giving them something to hold in their mouths helps redirect some of their energy and helps them remain calmer than they might otherwise be. This is not any type of formal retrieve or carry behavior; this is simply offering the dog something to put in his mouth to calm him, similar to offering a baby a pacifier. If the baby eventually spits out the pacifier, it is no big deal, and the same applies to a dog who is offered a "binkie" to carry to help him remain calm. Anything the dog is willing to carry that isn't dangerous can be used for this management technique. If he wants to pick up a stick on his walk and carry it, he can as long as he doesn't chew it up and risk getting slivers in his mouth and throat. If he gets tired of carrying it and spits it out, that's OK too. You aren't telling him to pick up the stick and carry it, so he isn't performing a behavior on cue; when he spits it out he isn't disobeying you. He is simply being a dog that has instincts to carry things in his mouth and is carrying something he found. He can quit carrying it whenever he wants to quit. If he has a favorite toy he likes to carry around at home, you can carry that along on your walks and offer it to him to carry if he wants to and quietly pick it up when he drops it. Some sporting dogs are calmer passing other dogs or people if they are also focusing on holding something in their mouths, so having a "puppy pacifier" handy can be useful. Again, this isn't a behavior you are teaching him to perform; it is a behavior that is part of his innate behavioral repertoire that may come in handy in exciting situations. If your dog doesn't naturally want to carry things in his mouth, that's OK, too. If you try to force him to carry something he doesn't want to carry, you will be exciting him even more and making the situation worse.

A favorite soft toy makes the perfect dog binkie for Susie.

A huntin' we will go

Sporting dogs are, at heart, hunters. They love to use their noses, eyes, and minds to find things. Engaging your dog in a hunting game is a powerful bonding activity for the two of you. Hunting with your dog doesn't have to involve guns or killing other animals; you can hunt anything that your dog is willing to put effort into obtaining. A tennis ball, tug toy, chew toy stuffed with treats, a favorite person, a pheasant wing, or a training bumper are just a few things your dog might enjoy hunting with you to find.

With a little pre-planning, you can use this game to reward good behavior on walks. Go out without your dog and hide a toy or treats somewhere along your walking route. Later, as you approach that area with your dog, ask him to perform a behavior or two (e.g., eye contact, sit, walk on loose leash, etc.). If your dog doesn't perform the behavior correctly, simply keep going on your walk and come back later to get the item you left. If he performs the behavior correctly, immediately praise him and release him to find his reward. Ask him "Where is your (whatever you hid)?" in an excited voice, so he knows he now has permission to sniff around and hunt. Participate in the hunt yourself by pointing out the general direction of the item, wiggling the grass, looking intently around, and basically acting like a dog on the hunt as well. Encourage your dog to move toward the item and when he finds it, praise him and let him eat his treats or enjoy his toy for a bit. If he wants to carry the toy when you continue walking, let him; if he drops it or isn't interested in carrying it, just quietly pick it up and carry it yourself.

A few safety tips for this game are important to keep in mind. If you use any type of food for this game, be sure that insects or other animals aren't going to get all over the food or that the food won't become unsafe being left out in the weather for awhile (raw treats are not a good choice for this game). If insects or animals are a possible threat to your hidden item, hide it up out of the reach of your dog, so that you must get it for him once he finds it. Then you can knock all the ants off if you need to before allowing your dog to eat the treat or play with the treat-stuffed toy.

Also, be sure your dog doesn't overheat if he decides to carry his precious hunt treasure on your walk. Even in cold weather, an excited working dog can generate considerable body heat and the primary way dogs get rid of internal heat is through panting. Carrying things impedes a dog's ability to pant, so you may need to take the item from your dog after a few minutes to keep him safe. You can give it back to him to carry in short spurts if he really enjoys carrying it. And to keep your dog guessing, never play this game in the exact same spot two times in a row and don't play every single time you go for a walk. He should never know for sure when or where this crazy hunting game might pop up. That unpredictability will keep him working hard for you because he won't be able to predict if his reward for any given behavior will be to go hunting with you.

Training exercises

Rapid fire fetch
Exercise Goal: Your sporting dog will bring back a toy when you throw it.

This training exercise is a very basic retrieve that is appropriate for teaching your dog to play fetch in the yard. The dog is not expected to formally deliver his object to you, but rather to simply come close enough to you that you can reach the item fairly easily. If the dog drops the item near you, there is no negative consequence. This is not a formal obedience retrieve or a hunting retrieve. Once your dog catches on to the game, you can also use it as a way to get more exercise out of play time for both you and your dog!

1. For this exercise, it is easiest to start inside in a fairly small room without a lot of furniture or breakable objects. If you have access to a room like this for initial training, you don't have to put your dog on leash for the first few steps. If you prefer to start your training outside, get a 50-foot

piece of nylon rope and a clasp and make a long line that you can use to control your dog in a larger space. You can buy the supplies at your local hardware store and use duct tape to tightly secure the clasp to the end of the line. You will *never* use this line to bring your dog to a sudden halt, but it will allow you to gently reel your dog back to you if he decides he wants to try to run away after grabbing his toy.

A piece of soft nylon rope, a clasp, and some duct tape are all you need to make an inexpensive long line of any length to use when training your dog.

2. You will also need two or three identical items that can be used for retrieving. Most dogs will readily fetch a tennis ball or similar-sized solid rubber ball, but others prefer to retrieve soft toys or actual training bumpers. The key to success with this training is to have two or three *identical* items to use in your early training sessions. If you buy doggie tennis balls, be sure they are all the same color and brand. Different dyes smell (and probably taste) different, so a red tennis ball might not be as desirable to your dog as a yellow one. Your dog should not be able to see, hear, smell, taste, or feel any difference between the items you use to teach this exercise. You will be trading items of exactly equal value during the initial training sessions, so his enthusiasm for retrieving one should be just as high as for retrieving the other. Once he catches on to bringing items back to you, you won't have to be so particular about the toys you use, but in the initial training phase, use identical items. A new tube of tennis balls reserved just for training is perfect if your dog likes them; they will be the same color, texture, age, and smell.

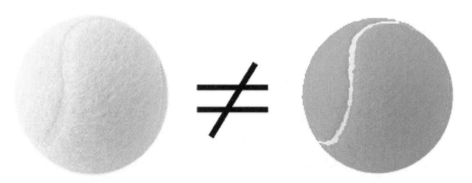

Although these two tennis balls may seem the same to us, our dogs will likely notice the differences in color, smell, and, quite possibly, taste. Using truly identical objects to start this training will make the process go more quickly.

3. With your dog either confined in a small room or on a long line outside, put one ball (or toy of your dog's choice) in your pocket and show him the other one. Make a big deal out if it, talk to it in an excited way, let him see it, then toss it just a few feet away from you and let your dog go get it. As soon as he picks up the ball, call his name enthusiastically, and start backing away from him. You want to encourage him with your body language and voice to come toward you; backing away from him also encourages him to move toward you in chase. If you tossed the ball a few feet away, he doesn't have to travel very far to get close to you, so it should be easy to get him within an arm's length of you. If you are outside where your dog has more room to run, use the long line to keep him from running away. Pick up the long line before you start backing away and reel him in with the rope while you call him and back away. It is particularly important to toss the ball just a few feet away to start so your dog doesn't generate much speed before you ask him to come back to you. If he is running too fast before you pick up the rope, you may hurt your dog's neck and spine and get severe rope burns on your hands when you try to stop him. If your dog won't bring a ball back to you when he is only a few feet away, he definitely isn't going to bring it back when he is far away from you.

4. When your dog is just within arm's reach, take the second ball out of your pocket and show it to him. Ask him if he wants the second ball in an excited voice and toss it in the air a couple of times to focus his attention on the new ball. Usually at this point, he will forget about the ball in his mouth and drop it near you. When that happens, immediately throw the second ball a few feet away and then pick up the first ball. Your dog should chase the second ball and, as soon as he picks that one up, call his name in an excited voice and start backing up. Keep the first ball hidden in your hand or behind your back until your dog is once again within an arm's length of you, then toss the ball you are holding in the air, get his attention on that one, and when he drops the one he is holding, throw

the one you are holding. Repeat this sequence a half dozen times, then pick up both balls and end the game.

5. If your dog tries to avoid you, work in a smaller space or on a shorter line until your dog will come willingly, if for no other reason than he has no other place he can go. Repeating this exchange will teach your dog that coming back to you doesn't end his retrieving fun, but, in fact, makes the fun continue because you will throw another item for him and continue to play.

6. As your dog becomes more reliable coming to you, begin to slowly increase the distance you throw the ball for him. If you are working inside, put him on a long line when you take him outside the first few times in case you need to help him understand that he needs to bring the ball back in this new environment. Keep the 80% rule in mind to help you know when it is appropriate to add more distance to your throws.

7. When your dog is reliably bringing the ball back to you, you can add in an element of self control if you desire, simply by asking your dog to sit and wait for you to tell him to go fetch his ball. Start with your dog sitting beside you, with your hand firmly holding his collar. Bend your knees slightly to help you keep your balance in case your dog tries to pull you over instead of calmly waiting to be released. Slowly and calmly roll his ball a few inches in front of him. Continue to hold his collar and wait for him to quit straining to get to his ball. As soon as he relaxes, release him to get his ball and call him back to you when he picks it up. Trade him by throwing the second ball as soon as he drops the first one. Let him go immediately to get the second ball; that immediate release to do another retrieve is his reward for exhibiting patience and sitting before retrieving the first ball. This game is very similar to Patience is a virtue in Chapter 9, except that in this game, your dog has to hold his sit position and relax before he can retrieve. Slowly increase the amount of time before you release him to get his ball to teach him more patience. Be sure to start varying how many times he must sit before you send him to retrieve his ball as compared to sending him immediately for it. If you always alternate a sit with an immediate release, he will soon learn this pattern and start to anticipate what you are going to ask him to do. Keep him guessing to keep his skills sharp and keep him listening to you.

Hold and give
Exercise Goal: Your sporting dog will hold an object on cue and release it on cue.

Although sporting dogs naturally know how to carry things in their mouths, it is handy to teach them to hold items on cue and release them on cue. Once your dog understands how to hold and give, you can teach him to help you with simple tasks, like picking up an item off the floor and bringing it to you, and to give you anything he has in his mouth even though you don't have anything to exchange for it.

1. For this training, it is useful to start with a toy your dog really likes that is small enough for your dog to hold comfortably in his mouth, but long

enough for you to be able to get ahold of it without sticking your fingers in your dog's mouth. The toy must also be somewhat soft; you want your dog to be able to comfortably hold the toy without any risk of hurting his mouth or chipping a tooth while you are playing with him. If you don't already have an appropriate toy to use, try braiding three old socks or three strips of fleece material together. Tie knots at both ends to keep the braid in place and see if you can get your dog interested in this toy. Keep your "hold-and-give" toy away from your dog when you aren't training this exercise to help the training go more quickly. Absence makes the heart grow fonder, so if your dog only has access to his favorite toy when you are training this exercise, he will be more eager to grab it and that will make the training go more quickly. Use the same toy for this exercise until your dog is fluent in taking, holding, and giving the toy up on cue. At that point, you can begin to use other items.

This Clumber Spaniel's long stick toy makes the perfect hold-and-give training toy to use for this exercise.

2. Start this exercise with your dog on-leash in a quiet, calm environment. Have tasty treats in your pocket or in a bowl nearby so your dog won't be distracted by them. Sit or step on the end of the leash so he can't decide to walk away while you are training, but leave enough slack in the leash so he can move around and grab at the toy. Your dog can be in any position to start this training.

3. Get your dog excited about his toy. Encourage him to take the toy by moving it slowly around on the ground like a bunny, talking in an exciting manner, teasing him a little with it to get his interest piqued, and showing great interest in the toy yourself. Your goal is to get your dog to take the toy firmly in his mouth. This isn't a forced, compulsory take on command (one where you physically make the dog take whatever item you want him to hold, whether he wants to take it or not), but rather

a fun take that the dog does of his own free will. If you can't get your dog to take the toy on his own, try a different toy. Also, be sure you are getting into the spirit of the game yourself; don't loom over your dog, get frustrated or angry if he doesn't take it right away, or be too rough when you are playing with him. Your dog must be relaxed enough to play for this training.

4.   The split second he takes the item in his mouth, tell him "Good take!" as you slide a hand gently under his chin to keep his mouth shut. Tip his head back just slightly to help him keep the object in his mouth and tell him "Good hold!" and stroke him on the top of his head in a long, slow stroke. Only ask him to hold the item for one second to begin with. Even though he might be holding his favorite toy, you are now controlling how long he must hold it, so he may try to spit it out right away. Start out with very short holds, and, using the 80% rule, gradually build up how long your dog holds the item over successive training sessions. Use only a slight upward pressure under his chin to keep the toy in his mouth; avoid grabbing the top of his muzzle and holding his mouth shut with both hands. For many dogs, this is similar to the type of correction they may have received at some point for nipping and may make it uncomfortable to keep ahold of the toy; as a result, the dog may start to actively fight holding the toy.

5.   After one second, grab a treat and offer him the treat while taking your hand out from under his chin. If you have played the Quid Pro Quo game with your dog already, you can use the cue you used in that game to let your dog know he should release his toy now. If you haven't worked on that game, tell your dog "Good give!" as he spits out the toy to take the treat. You are simply making an exchange to get him release his toy.

6.   If he won't release his toy for the treat, you need to up the ante with the treat. You must offer him a treat that is more valuable to him than the toy he is holding if you want him to drop the toy and take the treat. If you can't find a more valuable treat for the exchange, use a less valuable toy the next time you train. You may have to experiment to find the correct balance between the toy and the treat to get your dog to quickly make the exchange.

7.   As your training progresses, you will notice your dog taking his toy more quickly and holding it with less help from you. At this point, you can start telling him "Take it" right before he grabs the toy, followed by "Hold it." Keep your hand near his chin so you can quickly help him hold the toy if he tries to spit it out before you are ready for him to give it back to you. Using the 80% rule, gradually move your hand away from his chin in 1 inch increments, until you no longer need to put your hand near him to remind him to hold his toy. If at any point he spits the toy out too soon, simply repeat the exercise and put your hand under his chin to remind him what he is supposed to do, then try again without your hand cue. Praise him quietly and calmly for holding his toy; if you get too excited with your praise, he may get excited too and spit out the toy. Start fading the play that is used to get him to take his toy. By this time, he should

understand the behavior well enough that he is anticipating what you are going to ask him to do and doesn't need the extra help to pick up the toy.

8. You can also start telling your dog "Give it" just before you offer him his treat in exchange for the toy. Once he starts to release the toy on cue, begin to delay the presentation of the treat until after he has released his toy. At this point, the treat becomes a reward for dropping the toy, rather than a bribe to get him to release it. If your dog doesn't drop the toy right away to earn his treat, don't repeat the cue or use the treat to get him to drop it. Simply wait quietly for him to figure out he needs to release the toy before he gets his treat, then reward him as soon as he drops it.

9. If your dog absolutely refuses to drop his toy, don't try to pull it out of his mouth. From your dog's point of view, you are playing a game with him. Pulling it away from him will encourage him to hold on more tightly and, if he does try to open his mouth to release it, you are pulling against his incisors and may damage his teeth. Instead, gently twist the toy toward the back of your dog's mouth. You aren't trying to hurt him or choke him by doing this, but making the toy more difficult to hold. Reflexes usually take over and the dog will spit the toy out on his own. Never risk breaking teeth or physically hurting your dog to get him to release his toy though. If you can't get him to give up his toy safely, walk away from him and ignore him. Eventually he will drop the toy and you can pick it up and put it away. Next training session, use a less valuable toy and/or a more valuable treat to get him to give his toy to you.

10. Once your dog is fluent with all three cues, you can begin to substitute other toys or items for his favorite toy. A ball is harder to work with if your dog refuses to release it because you will need to stick your fingers in his mouth to move the ball around and there is no way for you to grab it securely. Leave the balls until your dog is really consistent at other objects that are easier for you to work with, so the likelihood that you will need to help your dog drop his ball is decreased. When you ask your dog to carry something in his mouth, always keep in mind the texture, taste, and safety of the item. Soft fabric items may absorb saliva, drying out your dog's mouth if you ask him to carry this type of item for long periods of time. Some brightly-colored toys undoubtedly have a distinct taste and smell to them that may be displeasing to your dog (similar to the bitter taste cake frosting can have if certain food colorings are used to excess). To keep your dog from getting injured or choking, don't use items that can break if your dog grasps them too tightly or that can be easily swallowed.

Teaching your sporting dog to hold and give items on cue opens up a whole new world of behaviors you can teach him to provide him physical and mental exercise.

A-tisket, a-tasket

Exercise Goal: Your sporting dog will hold a basket and carry small items in it.

1. You can give your dog a job to do once he knows how to take, hold, and give items on cue by finding a small basket with a handle on it that

you can use to have your dog carry items for you around the house. The basket should be small enough that it doesn't extend below your dog's elbows when he is walking, and the handle should be wide enough that he can comfortably and securely carry it behind his incisors. Wrap the middle of the handle in duct tape to protect the basket handle from wearing out from use; when the tape gets worn, simply replace it. After your dog is fluent holding his favorite toy and a few other objects, introduce your dog to holding the basket. If he is fluent performing the behaviors with his toy, he should quickly learn to take, hold, and give the basket. However, he will still need to learn how to walk with the basket bouncing against his chest.

2. Start the walking portion of this training with your dog on leash. Encourage him to stand up before you ask him to take the basket; this will make it much easier for him to take those first few steps. Stand facing your dog and ask him to take the basket and hold it. As soon as he does, take a couple steps backwards and encourage your dog to come to you. By using your voice and body, you should be able to get your dog to move forward toward you without pulling on his leash. If there is tension on the leash, it may put pressure on the basket and cause your dog to spit it out. As soon as he has taken a step or two toward you, stop, ask him to give you the basket, and then reward him. If you praise him too excitedly for moving, he may get excited and spit out the basket. If at any point your dog drops the basket before you ask him to give it to you, start over asking him to take the basket and make the moving portion easier for him. Some dogs take longer than others to figure out they can still walk even though there is something lightly touching their chests.

3. Continue having your dog come toward you until he is comfortable moving ten feet or more to catch up with you as you back away from him. At that point, you can start asking him to carry his basket while walking beside you. Stand at his side, ask him to take his basket, then take a step or two forward with him. When you stop, ask him to give you the basket before rewarding him. Using the 80% rule, gradually increase the distance he will walk while carrying his basket.

4. When your dog is fluent walking with his empty basket, you can begin to add weight to the basket. Consider how much weight your dog's breed was expected to carry if he were used in his traditional hunting role when deciding how much weight you can safely ask your dog to carry. A Curly-Coated Retriever could be used to retrieve geese from the water, while the smaller Cocker Spaniel was used on partridge and similar small birds, so a Curly can realistically be expected to carry more weight than a Cocker. Don't ask your dog to carry more weight in his basket than the game birds his breed was developed to retrieve. Very slowly build up the weight he carries for you, so he can build up his neck, jaw, and shoulder muscles. Also, keep in mind that sporting dogs were never asked to carry one particular item for extended periods of time. Typically, a downed bird might be carried for a few minutes at most while the dog brought

it back to the hunter. The dog was not expected to carry the bird all the way back home.

5.   Once your dog is comfortable with a little weight in his basket, you can start asking him to work for you around the house. For example, you can leave his basket by the back door and when you are ready to go out in the yard to do some yard work, you could drop your gardening gloves or a small pair of pruning shears in the basket and ask your dog to carry the basket outside for you. Leave a leash in his basket as well so you can quickly and easily put him on leash to make sure he comes with you instead of taking off in the yard, basket in tow. Your dog won't care that you really don't need him to carry these things for you—he will be thrilled to be working with you, using his oral instincts in a manner similar to the way his ancestors did when they carried birds back to the hunters, and you will be the envy of many other dog owners to have such a helpful dog!

You will never completely destroy a sporting dog's oral instincts. Instead of fighting against those instincts and constantly battling with your dog, put them to good use to provide your dog a little more exercise and a much more meaningful sporting dog life!

Conclusion

It is a truism to say that the dog is largely what his master makes of him. He can be savage and dangerous, untrustworthy, cringing and fearful; or he can be faithful and loyal, courageous and the best of companions and allies.

~ *Sir Ranulph Fiennes*
British explorer

Life with sporting dogs is always exciting and, at times, can be quite challenging. The instincts that allowed their ancestors to survive and thrive in harsh hunting environments are often in direct conflict with the comfortable urban environs most of us now share with our dogs. These instincts can present training challenges that might, at first, seem too difficult to overcome. By adopting a more sporting dog-centric view of the world and working with our dogs—rather than against them—we can teach our dogs how to behave more appropriately in our homes, without trying to make them into something they are not. The time you invest in training your sporting dog will not only result in more acceptable behavior from him, but also a stronger, more loving bond between the two of you. And that is definitely an investment worth making.

The bond shared between you and your sporting dog is a very special one. Be sure to make the most of it!

Appendix

Sporting Breeds Used to Assist Hunters by Locating and/or Retrieving Game

American Cocker Spaniel

American Water Spaniel

Barbet

Basenji

Belgian Short-Haired Pointer

Boykin Spaniel

Bracco Italiano

Braque d'Ariège

Braque d'Auvergne

Braque du Bourbonnais

Braque Dupuy

Braque Français de Grande Taille

Braque Français de Petite Taille

Braque Saint-Germaine

Brittany

Burgos Pointer

Cesky Fousek

Chesapeake Bay Retriever

Clumber Spaniel

Curly-Coated Retriever

Deutscher Langhaariger Vorstehhund

Deutscher Wachtelhund

Drentse Patrijshond

Drótszörü Magyar Vizsla

El Perro de Agua de Espagnol

English Cocker Spaniel

English Pointer

English Setter

English Springer Spaniel

Épagneul Bleu de Picardie

Épagneul Français

Épagneul Picard

Épagneul Pont-Audemer

Field Spaniel

Finnish Spitz

Flat-Coated Retriever

Gammel Dansk Hønsehund

German Short-Haired Pointer

German Wire-Haired Pointer

Golden Retriever

Gordon Setter

Grosser Münsterländer

Hertha Pointer

Hollandse Tulphond

Irish Setter

Irish Red and White Setter

Irish Water Spaniel

Kleiner Münsterländer Vorstehhund

Kooikerhondje

Labrador Retriever

Long-Haired Weimaraner

Niam-Niam

Norbottenspets

Norwegian Lundehund

Nova Scotia Duck Tolling Retriever

Old English Spaniel

Old Spanish Pointer

Perdigueiro Portugueso

Pointer

Poodle

Pudelpointer

Russian (Russkaja) Spaniel

St John's Water Dog

Slovensky Hruborsty Stavac

Spinone Italiano

Stabyhoun

Sussex Spaniel

Vizsla

Wire-Haired Vizsla

Weimaraner

Welsh Springer Spaniel

Wetterhound

Wire-Haired Pointing Griffon

Resources

Outside of a dog, a book is a man's best friend. Inside of a dog, it is too dark to read.

~ Groucho Marx
American comedian

Recommended reading and cited works

Aloff, Brenda. *Canine Body Language: A Photographic Guide.* Collierville, TN, Fundcraft, Inc., 2005. Comprehensive visual guide to all aspects of canine body language.

Antoniak-Mitchell, Dawn. *Terrier-Centric Dog Training: From Tenacious to Tremendous.* Wenatchee, WA, Dogwise Publishing, 2013. Management and training techniques useful for working terriers.

Arkwright, William. *The Pointer and His Predecessors.* London, UK, Humphreys, 1906. Includes a discussion of the role gun development played on gun dog development.

Barry, Jim, Mary Emmen and Susan Smith. *Positive Sporting Dogs: Clicker Training for Sporting Breeds.* Waltham, MA, Sunshine Books, Inc., 2007. Complete training program for field work based on positive reinforcement techniques.

Bishop, Sylvia. *It's Magic: Training Your Dog with Sylvia Bishop.* United Kingdom, Sylvia Bishop, 1985. Unique, hands-on approach to training all types of dogs for Euro-style competitive obedience.

Cauis, Johannes. *Of English Dogs—The Diversities, the Names, the Natures, and the Properties.* First edition London, UK, Richard Johnes, 1576, as reprinted, Warwickshire, UK, Vintage Dog Books, 2005. Reprint of one of the earliest descriptions of dogs known in the English language.

Coppinger, Raymond and Lorna Coppinger. *Dogs: A New Understanding of Canine Origin, Behavior, and Evolution.* Chicago, IL, University of Chicago Press, 2001. Outstanding presentation of issues relating to the canine-human bond.

Coren, Stanley. *The Intelligence of Dogs.* New York, NY, Bantam Books, 1994. Easy-to-read explanation of the various ways to assess canine intelligence.

Cummins, Bryan D. *Colonel Richardson's Airedales: The Making of the British War Dog School 1900—1918.* Calgary, Alberta, CAN, Detselig Enterprises Ltd., 2003. Detailed description of the development of the British military canine program, including the use of various dog breeds.

Dalziel, Hugh. *British Dogs—Their Varieties, History, Characteristics, Breeding, Management and Exhibition.* First edition, London, UK, Alfred Bradley, 1888, as reprinted, London, UK, Ersham Press, 2007. Reprint of late eighteenth-century book describing contemporary dog breeds.

Delta Society. *Professional Standards for Dog Trainers: Effective, Humane Principles.* Renton, WA, Delta Society, 2001. Standard of professional conduct designed to provide a framework for effective, humane dog training.

Donaldson, Jean. *The Culture Clash.* Berkeley, CA, James & Kenneth Publishers, 1996. Easy-to-read exploration of why humans and canines often have communication problems and how to communicate in a more effective way with your dog.

Dunbar, Ian. *Barking.* Berkeley, CA, Center for Applied Animal Behavior, 1986. Easy-to-read primer on barking problems.

Franklin, Adrian. *Animals and Modern Cultures: A Sociology of Human-Animal Relations in Modernity.* London, UK, Sage Publications, 1999. Overview of present-day relationships with animals.

Ganley, Dee. *Changing People Changing Dogs: Positive Solutions for Difficult Dogs.* Chipping Campden, UK, Learning About Dogs, Ltd., 2006. Information on assessing the causes for canine behavioral problems and clicker-based behavioral modification plans.

Garrett, Susan. *Ruff Love.* Chicopee, MA, Hadley Printing Company, Inc., 2002. Very detailed program to develop a strong working relationship between dog and handler.

Haggerty, Captain. *How to Teach Your Dog to Talk.* New York, NY, Simon & Schuster, 2000. Trick training in easy-to-follow format.

Hall, Libby. *Postcard Dogs.* London, UK, Bloomsbury Publishing, 2004. Interesting historical collection of late-eighteenth and early-nineteenth century dog images, including many sporting breeds.

Hoffmann, L. *Das Buch vom gesunden und kraken Hund.* Wein, Osterrich, Verlag con Moritz Perles, 1902. (In German.) A description of German dog breeds.

Jensen, P., Ed. *The Behavioural Biology of Dogs.* Trowbridge, UK, 2008. Collection of articles written by international experts on canine behavior.

Lee, Rawdon. *A History & Description of the Modern Dogs of Great Britain & Ireland (Sporting Division).* Reprint of 1893 ed., London, UK, Adamant Media Corporation,

2006. Detailed descriptions and anecdotes of the development and historical use of British sporting dog breeds.

Leighton, Robert. *Dogs and All About Them.* London, UK, Cassell and Company Ltd., 1910. Interesting turn-of-the-century historical perspective on various dog breeds, including sporting breeds.

Lindsay, Steven. *Handbook of Applied Dog Behavior and Training: Vol. 1 Adaptation and Learning.* Ames, IA, Iowa State Press, 2000. Scholarly work on research and findings related to how canines evolved and how the canine brain works.

Lindsay, Steven. *Handbook of Applied Dog Behavior and Training: Vol. 2 Etiology and Assessment of Behavior Problems.* Ames, IA, Iowa State Press, 2000. Scholarly work on research related to the physical basis and identification of canine behavioral problems.

Lindsay, Steven. *Handbook of Applied Dog Behavior and Training: Vol. 3 Procedures and Protocols.* Ames, IA, Iowa State Press, 2000. Scholarly work on research and findings related to the theory of cynopraxis and behavioral modification.

London, Karen. *Feeling Outnumbered? How to Manage and Enjoy Your Multi-Dog Household.* Black Earth, WI, Dog's Best Friend Ltd., 2001. Useful ideas for successfully living with multiple dogs.

Morris, Desmond. *Dogs: The Ultimate Dictionary of Over 1,000 Dog Breeds.* North Pomfret, VT, Trafalgar Square Publishing, 2001. Well-illustrated and informative general reference book on dog breeds throughout the world.

Pryor, Karen. *Don't Shoot the Dog: The New Art of Teaching and Training.* Revised edition, New York, NY, Bantam Books, 1999. Revised edition of the classic work on operant conditioning and clicker training.

Pugnetti, Gino. *Cani.* Milan, IT, Mondadori Electa S.p.A., 2003. (In Italian). Interesting contemporary reference book of European dog breeds, including sporting breeds.

Reid, Pamela. *Excel-erated Learning: Explaining in Plain English How Dogs Learn and How Best to Teach Them.* Berkeley, CA, James & Kenneth Publishers, 1996. Learning theory in lay terms for quick and easy application.

Riddle, Maxwell. *Dogs Through History.* Fairfax, VA, Denlinger's Publishers, 1987. General work on the evolution of canines and the canine-human bond.

Ritvo, H. *The Animal Estate: The English and Other Creatures in the Victorian Age.* Cambridge, MA, Harvard University Press, 1987. Interesting information about the beginning of the "pet age."

Rogerson, John. *How to Get Your Dog to Play.* United Kingdom, Coronation Press Limited, 2004. Useful booklet with innovative ways to encourage your dog to play with you.

Rogerson, John. *The Dog Vinci Code.* United Kingdom, John Blake Publishing, Ltd., 2010. Engaging and unique approach to common behavioral and dog training problems.

Rugaas, Turid. *Barking: The Sound of a Language.* Wenatchee, WA, Dogwise Publications, 2008. Interesting perspective on dog-to-dog vocal communications.

Rugaas, Turid. *On Talking Terms with Dogs: Calming Signals.* Wenatchee, WA, Dogwise Publications, 2006. Fascinating detailed examination of dog-to-dog non-vocal communications and how to use the same types of signals to communicate with your dog.

Schade, Victoria. *Bonding with Your Dog: A Trainer's Secrets for Building a Better Relationship.* Hoboken, NJ, Wiley Publishing, Inc., 2009. Exercises designed to help build a stronger relationship between you and your dog.

Scott, John and John Fuller. *Genetics and the Social Behavior of the Dog.* Chicago, IL, University of Chicago Press, 1965. Groundbreaking scientific study into the social development of dogs.

Serpell, James. *In the Company of Animals: A Study of Human-Animal Relationships.* Cambridge, UK, University Press, 1996. Exploration of the varied roles animals play in modern life.

Spector, Morgan. *Clicker Training for Obedience.* Waltham, MA, Sunshine Books, Inc., 1999. Comprehensive manual on clicker training for competitive obedience from Novice through Utility.

Stifel, Robert. *The Dog Show: 125 Years of Westminster.* New York, NY, Westminster Kennel Club, 2001. Interesting insights into premier US dog show, with historical information on various early Westminster winners.

Tuan, Yi-Fu. *Dominance and Affection: The Making of Pets.* New Haven, CT, Yale University Press, 1984. Philosophical work on the reasons we keep animals as pets.

Yunck, Adele. *The Art of Proofing.* Ann Arbor, MI, Jabby Productions, 2008. Useful resource for improving reliability and generalizing competitive obedience behaviors that can also be adapted for use with everyday obedience behaviors.

Videos and DVDs

Kalnajs, Sarah. *The Language of Dogs: Understanding Canine Body Language and Other Communication Signals.* Wenatchee, WA, Dogwise Publishing, 2006. Video presentation of canine communication and behavior with accompanying commentary.

Nelson, Leslie. *Really Reliable Recall.* Manchester, CT, Healthy Dog Productions, 2004. Straightforward method for teaching your dog to come when called in an emergency.

Selected Internet Resources

American Kennel Club. http://www.akc.org Largest all-breed dog registry in the United States, also offering various competitive activities for sporting dogs. (8/21/13).

Clothier, Suzanne. "He Just Wants to Say Hi!" http://suzanneclothier.com/the-articles/he-just-wants-say-hi A must-read for all dog owners who take their dogs out in public. (8/21/13).

Dogfoodadvisor.com. http://m.vetmed.iastate.edu/vetapps/AdultBodyCondChart.pdf Provides information and links to canine weight and nutrition topics, including the Purina Body Condition System chart. (8/21/13).

Gundogsupply.com. http://www.gundogsupply.com/dummies.html Reliable source for various training supplies, including training bumpers. (8/21/13).

J & J Dog Supplies. http://www.jjdog.com Well-established source of competitive obedience training supplies. (8/21/13).

North American Versatile Hunting Dog Association. http://www.navhda.org/ Non-profit whose purpose is to foster, promote, and improve versatile hunting dog breeds in North America. (8/21/13).

Positive Gun Dogs of Minnesota. http://www.positivegundogsmn.com Seminars, classes, educational resources, training and behavior services. (12/17/13).

Premier Dog Products. http://www.premier.com/store/ Great source for high quality dog training products and toys. (8/21/13).

United Kennel Club. http://www.ukcdogs.com/Web.nsf/WebPages/HRC/Home Nationwide registry offering various competitive activities for sporting dogs. (8/21/13).

Wwwmagyarvizslalu on Youtube.com. http://www.youtube.com/watch?v=ZSm5-e7uga4 (Are you fit enough for a Vizsla?) Thought-provoking video for anyone considering buying a sporting dog. (8/21/13).

ABOUT THE AUTHOR

Dawn Antoniak-Mitchell, Esq., MPA, CPDT-KSA, CBCC-KA started training dogs when she was in 4-H. Since leaving the practice of law to become a full-time dog trainer, Dawn has helped hundreds of dog owners understand their dogs better and learn how to train them, while still respecting their unique needs as dogs. She has worked as a behavioral consultant for a national dog food company and owns BonaFide Dog Academy LLC in Omaha, NE.

Dawn is a Certified Professional Dog Trainer—Knowledge and Skills Assessed (CCPDT), a Certified Behavioral Consultant—Canine Knowledge Assessed (CCPDT), an AKC obedience and rally obedience judge, an AKC Canine Good Citizen evaluator, a World Cynosport (formerly APDT) rally obedience judge, a CDSP obedience judge and has served as a Delta Society Pet Partner evaluator. She has been published in local, regional, and national publications, including *Top Tips from Top Trainers,* published by the Association of Pet Dog Trainers, and has been interviewed internationally on

Dawn and her Dalmatian Melody Crystal Fire Hot Spot "Ember."

several training topics. Dawn is the author of *Terrier-Centric Dog Training: From Tenacious to Tremendous,* published by Dogwise Publications in 2012. She has appeared as guest author on several dog book discussion lists. Dawn is also a lecturer and advocate for the Americans with Disabilities Act and service dogs; she has been invited to medical schools and disabled veterans' conferences to speak on the ADA, the rights and responsibilities of service dog owners, and psychiatric service dog training, allowing her to combine her legal expertise and her dog training experience in a unique way to help others.

Over the years, Dawn has successfully trained and competed with dogs from the Sporting, Non-Sporting, Herding, and Terrier groups in a wide range of activities, including conformation, obedience, rally obedience, agility, tracking, scent work, earthdog tests, musical freestyle, and weight pulling, achieving national rankings with many of her dogs. Her dogs have been regularly featured in local and national print and video productions. She also volunteers with her dogs in reading therapy programs in local schools. Her Curly-Coated Retriever Barnum was the first CCR in the country to earn an AKC rally obedience title at each of the three levels of competition, as well as the first to earn World Cynosport (formerly APDT) rally obedience titles in Levels 1 and 2.

Photo credits

Dawn Antoniak-Mitchell (photographer) and Border Collie Gabriel, Dalmatian Ember, Jack Russell Terriers Jinx and Glitch and Curly-Coated Retriever Barnum; Andy, Grace, Luke, Shay, and Bethany Bailey and Vizslas Belle and Bode; Kaija Braid and Sussex Spaniels Bonnie, Clyde, and Jack, Sussex Spaniel puppies Mia, Ken, Osku, Cassie, Tucky, and Kira and Curly-Coated Retriever Tuuri; Chuck Casanova and German Wirehaired Pointer Outlaw; Dena Bream and Curly-Coated Retriever Poppy. Jeff Bream (photographer) and Curly-Coated Retriever Eli. Kristal Hayes (photographer), Izzy Hayes and Curly-Coated Retrievers Wesley and Boomer. Doris Hodges (photographer) and Curly-Coated Retriever Keeper; Regan Hulbert and English Setters Eva and Dezi; Virginia Huxley and English Springer Spaniel Lainie; Ewa Knuplerz and Clumber Spaniels Thelma, Vis, and Taboo; Chuck and Karen Meyer and Labrador Retriever KoKo; Jeff Mitchell and Jack Russell Terriers Lizzie B. and Curly-Coated Retriever Shocker; Robin K. Nelson DVM and German Wirehaired Pointer Calley; Joe Plugge and Weimaraner Titus. Janna Puurunen (photographer) and Field Spaniel Caino; Karen Stevens and Golden Retriever Keagan; Linda Stevenson and Labrador Retriever Maya; Sandra Stubbe-van Roest and Field Spaniel Nova. Hannie Warendorf (photographer), and Wies Boermans and Flat-Coated Retrievers Misty, Susie, and Denzel.

Index

Also available from Dogwise Publishing

Go to www.dogwise.com for more books and ebooks.

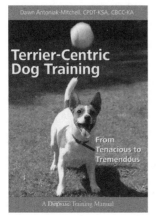

Terrier-Centric Dog Training
From Tenacious to Tremendour
Dawn Antoniak-Mitchell

All kinds of dogs have a number of hard-wired traits bred into them. Hounds love to follow their noses, Retrievers love to fetch and Herding dogs love to herd. With few exceptions, these are pretty harmless activities and don't stand in the way of training. Terriers, however, were bred to hunt and kill vermin independently, digging underground and barking excitedly, almost impervious to pain. Let's see...just a few challenges to overcome in training: strong prey drive, independence, feistiness, digging, barking, the list goes on. In Terrier-Centric Dog Training, author Dawn Antoniak-Mitchell takes up the challenge to help terrier owners train their dogs by making sure they understand the instincts bred into terriers and what the most effective training and management techniques are to use when working with a "natural born killer." You can train your terrier, but just don't let him loose off-leash in a park full of squirrels!

The Clicked Retriever
Lana Mitchell

The retrieve is one of the most difficult skills for most dogs to master in competitive obedience. It is difficult because it involves a long series of steps that the dog must learn in order to retrieve the object successfully. More and more trainers are realizing that teaching a complex series of behaviors like this is most easily done through the use of clicker training—using the same techniques used by large animal trainers working with whales, dolphins and elephants. *The Clicked Retriever* teaches you step-b-step how to clicker train your dog to do a solid, enthusiastic and reliable retrieve. Learning no-force techniques builds trust between you and your dog, makes training more enjoyable for both of you and sets you up for life long training success built on scientific principles, respect and fun.

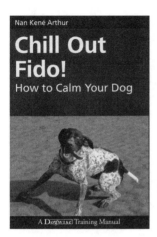

Chill Out Fido!
How to Calm Your Dog
Nan Arthur

Calm your canine wild child

Does your dog go bonkers when the doorbell rings or when you grab the leash to take him for a walk? If you find your dog is often difficult to control, you are not alone! Getting your dog to calm down and relax is one of the most common challenges pet parents face. This two-part book will help you first identify the factors that cause this kind of behavior in dogs, then it provides you with eleven key training exercises to teach your dog how to calm down, pay attention to you, relax, and respond to every day situations with confidence and composure. Chill Out will show you how to help your dog become the great dog you always knew he could be.

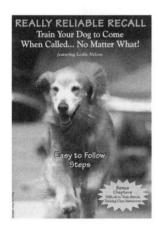

Really Reliable Recall
Train Your Dog to Come When Called... No Matter What! DVD
Leslie Nelson

Leslie Nelson's *Really Reliable Recall* DVD shows easy to follow steps to train your dog to come when called, especially when it really counts—in an emergency! Learn how to build trust and ensure safety. Once trained, the recall works immediately in any situation, no matter what your dog is doing. He doesn't think, he doesn't decide, he just comes to you. This dog training DVD also contains chapters focusing on difficult to train breeds as well as chapters that can be used by dog trainers during class instruction.

Dogwise.com is your source for quality books, ebooks, DVDs, training tools and treats.

We've been selling to the dog fancier for more than 25 years and we carefully screen our products for quality information, safety, durability and FUN! You'll find something for every level of dog enthusiast on our website www.dogwise.com or drop by our store in Wenatchee, Washington.